The Bomb Life

My Brand. My Terms.

Dear Rachel,

You are an inspiration! I'm so
glad I met you! I look
forward to growing & building together.

xox U,

CLAIRE SULMERS

Library of Congress Cataloging-in-Publication Data

Claire Sulmers
The Bomb Life
Edited by: Driandonna Roland
Published by: Fashion Bomb World, LLC

Library of Congress Control Number: 2016918825

ISBN: 978-0692812907
ISBN-10: 0692812903

Printed in the United States of America

Note: This book is intended only as a real life testimony of the life and times of Claire Sulmers. The information in this book is based on the author's experience. The author has tried to recreate events, locales and conversations from her memories of them. In order to maintain their anonymity, in some instances she has changed the names of individuals, companies, and places. She may have changed some identifying characteristics and details such as physical properties, occupations and places of residence.

Author Photography by Derek Blanks

Table of Contents

Introduction 1

1   Yes, I went to Harvard 3

2   When Writing Found Me 19

3   Not So Nice; The Birth of Fashion Bomb Daily. . 33

4   From New York to Paris .51

5   The Nobody at Paris Vogue 79

6   The Business of Blogging 109

7   Looking the Part 125

8   Not Everyone Wants to See you Win. 133

9   Love and Business. 145

10 The New Frontier 167

11 Letters to my Younger Self. 185

Introduction

My maternal grandfather, Haisley Fletcher Newton, was a master tailor in Nassau, Bahamas. He made men's clothing, specifically suits, for the politicians and well-to-do in the community.

My paternal grandfather, Dalton Sylmé, was a master carpenter. Born in Haiti, he apprenticed for several years before moving to the United States and starting his own furniture company, the Dalton Sulmers Furniture Company. He changed his last name from Sylmé to Sulmers when he migrated to the States so that he could have a sweeter, more American sounding name.

This bold union of fashion, fluidity and entrepreneurship is my legacy.

I stand on their shoulders.

This is my story.

❧ 1 ❧

Yes, I went to Harvard

YES, I WENT to Harvard.

I never really thought I was Harvard material. Growing up, going to an Ivy League wasn't even a notion.

My Caribbean parents always put a huge emphasis on education. According to lore, my brother and I were reading by the age of 3. My mother, a school teacher, always had books around the house. Instead of watching Saturday morning cartoons and pouring deliciously sugary cereal into our mouths, my brother and I were carted off to piano lessons, dance lessons, and the museum. I gotta admit that when I was younger, I resented not being able to indulge in He-Man, She-Ra, and Jem on Saturday mornings. I groaned when we had to wake up early and go to music lessons. But I guess my mom had other plans.

When I was in fourth grade, she moved our family from Brooklyn, New York, down to Atlanta, Georgia, for several reasons. My father, who was an airplane pilot, was working for Eastern Airlines, which was based in Atlanta at the time. My mother also reasoned that we'd have more space to grow, fewer temptations, and perhaps better access to good schools. Living in New York now and understanding the high prices and politics associated with private schools, I definitely understand.

My brother and I applied to and tested for all the top schools in Atlanta: Lovett, Westminster, Pace, and Marist. We got into all the schools we applied for, but apparently Westminster was the best of the bunch. So there we went.

I remember driving up to the school, whose sprawling campus and copious trees were a far cry from the concrete public school I attended in Brooklyn. I walked into the lunchroom on the first day with butterflies in my stomach. Kids were pretty nice, as I was new, but I was painfully shy. I kept to myself until the bell rang and it was time for class.

Those first few weeks, I spent recess by myself, swinging on the swing set because we honestly didn't have access to such beautiful things in Brooklyn. Our recesses in Brooklyn consisted of jumping rope or playing tag on a concrete slab surrounded by a fence. In Georgia, we had trees, slides, swings, pogo sticks, books, and computers. When I wasn't swinging solo,

I would read Hans Christian Andersen fairy tales and write about secret gardens, replete with illustrations. My family lived 45 minutes away from my private high school, so I spent most weekends with my mom. To pass the time, I would apply makeup in the mirror, try on different outfits, and ask my mom how to sew. (I was a horrible pupil.)

I can say that it was around that time that I became interested in fashion. Perhaps it was out of boredom that I would try varied scarves on my head, slip on kimono-style gowns, and smear on lipstick in the mirror, dreaming of one day being a model. I started to tear through magazines like *Seventeen* and look through them for inspiration. The models were gorgeous but I was immediately aware that they looked nothing like me. The lithe, thin bombshells like Cindy Crawford, Christy Turlington, and Niki Taylor were far more glamorous than the bespectacled girl with chubby cheeks and cornrows who admired their every picture.

It was also around the end of elementary school and the beginning of junior high when I started to pay more attention to my clothing. I'm almost ashamed to admit then when I came to Westminster in fourth grade, I gave myself a uniform. Every Monday, I wore a red shirt and black pants. Every Tuesday, it was a floral shirt and shorts. And on and on. When you're young, you can sorta get away with that, but around age 12, things were changing.

The whole Atlanta move hadn't really worked out exactly how my parents had planned. It took my mom several years to find a job. And almost as soon as my family moved down to Atlanta, Eastern Airlines went bankrupt, leaving my father unemployed. Though my dad quickly found a new job at United Airlines, he was starting from the bottom, which meant he went from making a six-figure salary to little more than $30,000 a year. Times were tough.

I went to a rich school. The tuition for a year was $30,000 (though my brother and I attended on scholarship and received generous financial aid). The kids in my school, though never flashy, came from wealthy families and had nice things. Everyone wore Nike Air Max sneakers that cost $100. While guys could get away with wearing T-shirts and Umbro soccer shorts, girls wore Banana Republic T-shirts, shorts from the Limited, and Guess Jeans. If you look back now, the prices of those items are probably negligible compared to the Céline, Givenchy, and Dior kids wear these days. But it's all relative.

I begged my dad to get me a few of the items the other girls were wearing. So, one day, he took me to the mall and bought me one Banana Republic T-shirt, one pair of Limited jean shorts, and one pair of Guess Jeans. Because these were my prized possessions, I reserved them for special occasions, but undoubtedly ended up wearing them at least once, sometimes twice, a week.

I'll never forget, one day we were in gym class, changing in the locker room. A girl named Janet Sims was getting changed next to me and remarked, "Didn't you wear those jeans yesterday?" I replied, "What, those jeans? No. I have a few pairs." She smirked sarcastically and said, "Oh, right. Cuz I swore you wore those exact same jeans the other day." I whispered, "No," and kept getting dressed. The shame reverberated through my body.

I instantly felt embarrassed that my family couldn't afford to buy me more than one pair of Guess Jeans. I felt inferior. It was at that moment I decided that fashion would be my weapon, and my armor against bullies of the world like Janet Sims. Instead of being that girl who only had a few nice things, I would have so many nice things no one could say anything to me, make me feel less than, or try to diminish my value. And thus my true obsession with fashion began.

Thankfully the tide changed for my parents by the time I went to junior high school. My mom found a full-time teaching position after several years of substitute teaching and temp jobs. My father's career was moving at a rapid pace. We weren't rich, but we were doing better, and thus could spend on a few trifles.

In junior high in the '90s, it was all about the GAP. The GAP was EVERYTHING. GAP jeans, GAP shoes, GAP outfits. If you were fly, you shopped at the GAP. The kids in my school went to the GAP in Lenox mall, which is in the rich Buckhead area of town. They bought all the brand's fun blazers, skirt sets, and jeans full price. I lived on the other side of town, close to malls like Market Square and Northlake, both of which also had GAP stores. But unlike the GAPs in Buckhead, the people in my part of town couldn't afford the $99 blazers, so the really nice stuff typically went on super sale. My mom and I used to clean up, buying all my heart could desire at serious steals. The result? I'd go to school wearing all the latest and greatest from the GAP and instead of people saying, "Didn't you wear that already?" they would exclaim, "You always dress so cute!" and "You always have the cutest clothes!" How funny, people even thought I was rich because of the amazing clothes I wore to school every day. The feeling became intoxicating, and I became known as the girl who always looked good and was always put together, wearing the best outfits. Little did they know, I was buying everything for a serious bargain at the malls in Stone Mountain.

Junior high also signaled a change for me because my school received an influx of kids, and I finally had a larger group of friends — young boys and girls I felt I could relate to and be comfortable around. Perhaps I got carried away with being so excited with my new clothes and friends that I forgot about school that sixth grade year. My friends and I, instead of going to teachers' classrooms for help with our homework after school or actually DOING our homework, would go into the bathroom, apply lip gloss, tell jokes, perfect our cat eye, sing SWV songs, and make up dance routines. We were the class clowns, the ones who were rowdy, loud, and always had something silly to say.

I'll never forget: at the end of sixth grade we had an assembly recognizing people for outstanding achievements. At the end of the assembly, the principal called students to the stage who had gotten Honor Roll and awarded them with a certificate decorated with a gold seal. My school wasn't very diverse; out of 200 students per class, we had about 12 black kids. I was shocked by how few black kids were called onto the stage. In fact, only one African-American girl, Alexis, was on Honor Roll. (She later attended Harvard as well.)

I looked over to my friends, who had been making jokes the whole assembly. They seemed unfazed, and laughed and said, "Oh well, guess I'm not smart enough for Honor Roll." But I felt a tremendous amount of shame because I knew, deep inside, that I was.

I started applying myself. I began studying, doing my homework, and asking teachers for help when I didn't know what was going on. I eventually started to ace the regular classes. For seventh grade math, I got almost perfect scores on every test, just because I did my homework! I realized that the tests were just slight variations on the homework, so when it was time for any quiz or test, I was prepared. Once you master the regular classes, you are inducted into honor classes. By high school, I was in all honors classes (except science), and I did well in those also. From seventh grade until graduation, I was on Honor Roll every semester. I got my gold certificate.

I became an exceptional student, but perhaps it was the short skirts or seeming obsession with fashion, cheerleading, and socializing that made people think I wouldn't amount to much.

Around my junior year of high school, my college guidance counselor met with my parents and me to discuss college options. While Yale, Dartmouth, and Columbia were on my wish list, my guidance counselor suggested I go to Agnes Scott, a small, Southern women's college in Atlanta, citing that anything Ivy League was a "reach." Sure, I had the grades, and was also involved in the orchestra, French Club, Chess Club, Diversity Alliance, cheerleading, and tennis, but the Ivy League seemed unrealistic. My father wasn't far behind in setting sights lower than mine. His neighbor worked at Georgetown, and he suggested he could make a connection to get me in.

But then my brother, who was an undergraduate at Harvard, suggested I give the good old HU a shot.

My brother was more of your typical nerd. While I turned up at cheerleading practice and never missed a football game, my brother was a state-ranked flute player and pianist. He was known for his smarts and vivacious personality at our high school, to the point where I was simply known as "André's sister" for most of my freshman and sophomore year. (We are four years apart, so thankfully we were never in high school together!)

André told me, "Claire, Harvard has the best libraries in the world and the best education. It's fun, trust me." I was doubtful, and honestly, not that interested! He entreated me to come visit him to see, so one spring weekend, I did.

As I stepped onto Harvard Yard, I saw all these cool kids, dancing it up at a BBQ. That night, we went out to the Kong, and I had my first Scorpion Bowl, a punch bowl–sized chalice full of every type of liquor behind the bar, plus an added shot of tequila for extra potency. It was intoxicating for sure and had me stumbling through the streets of Cambridge (and throwing up in my brother's bathroom all night — believe it or not he cried when he saw me drunk, lying almost prone on his bathroom floor). To make it short, I had a fun time when I visited Harvard, and per my brother's suggestion, I applied — early — not thinking I would actually get in.

My brother also suggested I go over and above by meeting with Harvard's head recruiter for the Southeast. Just my luck, said recruiter came to my school for a college fair. I met her, chatted her up, and got her information.

I stayed in touch with her, and kept her updated as I won various awards or received any accolades. My brother also recommended I submit an extra credit essay to the recruiter, in addition to the essay I submitted as part of my application, which I did.

Then one sunny day in May, I came home from school to discover a letter from Harvard in the mailbox. My mind raced as I sat on the curb in front of my house and tore the envelope open. Then the bomb dropped: I got in!

I jumped up in the sky, pumped my fist, then ran down the driveway of my house to my car and hopped in! My mom wasn't home at the time (and this was before cell phones). I bumped Janet Jackson's "We Go Deep" as I traveled across town to go back to school and tell my friends.

As I drove to school, I saw my friends and revealed the news! To my slight dismay, they weren't that excited for me. Later that week, when I was sharing my good news with the cheerleading squad, one of my best friends, a Persian girl with a striking look, said, "You know you got in because you're black." Perhaps she didn't remember all the time I had spent in the library, or how I had managed to score Honor Roll every semester, while she just slid by. At any rate, I was excited about going to Harvard, and prepared myself the best I could.

So the PLAN was for me to work during the summer, save up some money for school, and be a responsible young adult, but I wasn't responsible at 18. I was always the type of girl who did what she wanted and went with the flow. Responsibilities were always far down on my list of priorities. That summer, I met a guy out at a club. He was a 22-year-old, unemployed musician who lived with his mom, but I didn't care! I was heady that I was dating an older guy; I spent most of my summer with him, eating out, going to clubs in downtown Buckhead, drinking, and partying it up!

When it came time to go to school, I was totally unprepared. Instead of saving money, I had spent it all living it up with my older beau (who had proposed to me; I ended up returning the ring within two weeks of getting acclimated at school). My dad yelled at me, asking me why I had spent my whole summer "gallivanting" instead of preparing for school. I had no answers. And it was this feeling of unpreparedness (and somewhat despair) I felt as I stepped onto Harvard Yard that first day of my freshman year.

Though I had gone away to summer camps, this was a huge leap. I was going up North, where everything seemed to move faster. Everyone seemed more sophisticated. And it was cold — something I'd have to get used to!

Thankfully my dad relented and bought me a computer; my mom and I had gone shopping to buy stuff for my dorm room. My dad gave me a small budget to buy sweaters and jackets. My parents came and set me up with my own bank account. And as they prepared to leave me, I started crying. I was scared. My mom asked why I was crying; I couldn't answer her. She said, "Listen. You're going to school with a bunch of dorks. These kids have no social skills. Don't worry." And with that, she left me.

Harvard took a lot of getting used to. My mother was right — I was going to school with a bunch of dorks! Most people I encountered on Harvard Yard were valedictorians and salutatorians, people who had gotten perfect SAT scores, and math whizzes with photographic memories.

I was none of the above.

I was a fun girl who liked to socialize and dress up. Many people on campus were pretty lame and had zero social skills. People I would meet and chat it up with at parties would look through me like glass when they saw me on campus the next day. (This would drive me crazy!)

For many months during my freshman year, I felt the admissions officers, who I had carefully and strategically courted, had made some sort of mistake. I wasn't valedictorian at my high school. I didn't have a photographic memory. I hadn't spoken at the Million Man March (as one my classmates had). I was just a girl from Stone Mountain, Georgia, with a crazy work ethic, attention to detail, and the ability to follow instructions. When my brother gave me tips on what to do to move my application to the top of the pile I did it, in addition to maintaining good grades and being involved in loads of extracurricular activities.

Freshman year was just about finding my groove. I gained the fabled Freshman 15, built a great group of friends, and even had a boyfriend. Because I had always gone to majority white schools, Harvard definitely wasn't a culture shock. I was used to this. But what I loved was having even more black people to talk to and socialize with. The girls I gravitated to all came from similar backgrounds: middle-class, first-generation immigrant families, whose parents all came to the States from an island and still had somewhat strict rules (and an accent to add extra emphasis). Once I had my group of Caribbean cuties, we were unstoppable. We went to parties together at Harvard, and also at Boston College, Boston University, Massachusetts Institute of Technology, and Tufts. The beauty of Boston is that it's a college town, so if you don't find what you want on your campus, you have your pick of other campuses to choose from! Freshman year was full of partying and drinking, but work called. I did pretty well my first year. I went to all my classes and sections, did my work, and finished the year up with A's and B's. But then, it was time to choose a major.

I always wanted to be a businesswoman, and for those interested in business, economics would be the route. (Harvard is a liberal arts school and doesn't have vocational majors like business or marketing.) But I wasn't a great mathematician, and numbers honestly bored me to tears. I hit up my brother, who had been instrumental in helping me along the way. He said, "Major in whatever you want to major in. After graduation, it won't matter. All job prospects will see is that you went to Harvard." So, I decided to merge two passions of mine: the French language and also African-American studies.

I always loved French. When I was 16, I did an exchange program and lived with a French family in the Northern town of Bayeux. After our homestay, we traveled the South of France. I was positively addicted after that first trip and proceeded to spend every summer afterwards in Paris, taking classes at the Sorbonne and making new friends.

African-American studies were also salient to me because of growing up in the South and going to a majority-white school all my life. I wanted to know more about my history — where I am from, where we are now, and where we were going.

No, my major had absolutely nothing to do with fashion. At the time, I didn't even know fashion could be a career. Yes, I enjoyed shopping. A lot. My revelation in junior high led to a crazy wardrobe full of ombre sweaters, bootcut jeans, and logo T-shirts.

My friend Elaine and I always used to stunt during school, wearing stiletto heels while navigating the cobblestones to class. While some of my classmates found it appropriate to meander around in pajamas or sweats, I rarely, if ever, did so. If I went for a sporty look, I was wearing a cute sweatsuit that had my name on it, with matching shoes. My outfits were color coordinated from my head down to my toes, sometimes with nail polish to match.

I knew I loved style, but didn't know where it would one day lead, or how my unconventional degree would play out one day in my career.

❧ 2 ❧

When Writing Found Me

WHILE AT HARVARD, I had uncovered my love for storytelling and writing. Also, through my African-American studies classes, I discovered how the media was very unkind to people of color. The producers weren't telling balanced stories, displaying the diversity of black people.

I wanted to be the one who changed that.

I dreamed of communicating the struggle of subjugated people to the world. I wanted to be the one to diversify the newsroom. I had completed two internships with major broadcasting companies, but even that was not enough to secure full-time employment after college in 2003, when the market was not friendly to recent graduates. After unsuccessfully trying to find a job in New York, my parents insisted I come home to figure things out. So I moved back to Atlanta, slightly dejected, and settled into life with my mother. I didn't have a job, seemed incapable of ever getting a job, and struggled to fill my time.

What was I to do in Atlanta? I hadn't the slightest idea. Thankfully one of my best friends from high school, Tanya, had never left home and was finishing up one last year at Georgia Tech. With Tanya, I was able to live the college life that my Ivy League school didn't supply. I was suddenly exposed, to my delight, to constant partying, tailgating, drinking at 9 a.m. before noon football games, and frat houses.

My job prospects were looking slim, and I reasoned: If I wanted to be a storyteller, why not write for magazines? One day, while perusing the magazine aisle in Kroger, I happened across an issue of *Upscale* magazine. The cover was enticing. I cracked it open and took a look at the masthead, and right there and then, decided to send in my resumé, cover letter, and writing sample. No, I wouldn't be working at CNN as a producer, but I would be potentially writing stories for a national magazine. To my surprise, after sending in my application materials, I got a call to come in and interview.

I wasn't super familiar with *Upscale*. During the interview, I angled to be a news intern, writing about the political and cultural issues of our day. But, just so happens, there was only one opening at the magazine:

in the fashion and beauty department. And thus my adventure in the worlds of fashion and beauty began.

This internship was completely unpaid. I didn't even get free lunch! But I didn't care. I busied myself packing and unpacking boxes for shoots and arranging beauty products in our beauty closet. I took a part-time job at Ann Taylor to cover my day-to-day expenses, and to make just enough to buy lunch every day from Chick-fil-A.

One day, my editor asked me to write a few captions for fashion articles. One of my first published pieces of writing was about a pair of Chanel shades. I typed, "Slip on a pair of these bold shades and be prepared to turn heads. The bright diamante double C on the wide tortoise arms of these rimless specs take logo loving to a whole new level..." I found that writing was kind of fun! And I was good at it.

My editors and pretty much everyone on staff noticed that I was good at it, too. We had weekly meetings, where we batted around ideas for what was hot and going on in culture. Our editor-in-chief increasingly asked me for my thoughts. He wanted to know what I felt was relevant and what was hot among recent graduates and the younger set.

As the weeks passed along, I started to get more and more responsibility. My small captions gave way to full-page articles. I was penning opinion pieces. By the final days of my internship, I was writing cover stories. I had found my calling.

During the last week of my internship, the magazine's editor-in-chief invited me into his office. He said, "You're very bright, and I'd like you to join our staff full time." I weighed the option of staying in Atlanta, versus moving to New York, where all of my friends lived post college. Every day I would keep in touch with them as they told me of all the parties and bottle popping in the Empire State. Besides, the object of my affection, a guy I had dated my senior year in college, was in New York.

I knew I loved writing, and figured that if I wanted to take it seriously, I would move to New York, home of the world's best magazines. After politely declining the offer, I asked my editor-in-chief if he could connect me with any of his friends he knew up North. I was moving to the Big Apple and was ready to take a bite.

I knew I couldn't live in New York without some form of income, so I researched which magazines offered paid internships post graduation (and didn't require school credit). There were only three: *New York* magazine, which paid $5.15 an hour; *Newsweek,* which paid $10 an hour; and *The Nation* magazine, which offered a stipend. I applied to all of them, and finally my Ivy League degree came in handy: I got all three internships.

Newsweek was only a summer internship, s
to choose between *The Nation* and *New York*. Because
I was going to be new to New York, I figured writing
for the weekly would be a cool gig. So to *New York*
magazine, I went.

I arrived in Gotham City in January 2004 — the
coldest month of the year (and apparently the coldest
winter in several years).

I had packed up all my boxes from Georgia, folded
all my Ann Taylor cashmere sweaters with care, and
sent them one way to my friend's apartment on the
Upper West Side. My freshman-year college roommate
lived in New York, and her mother, a generous woman
(who happened to be a journalist) opened their house
to me. My friend's brother had gone away for college
that year, and the apartment had an empty twin-sized
bed with my name on it. I remember talking to my
friend, Nadine, on the phone about the arrangement:
"Yes, you can stay with us, but you just have to buy
your own food." "Not a problem." I smiled, not real-
izing what a gift a rent-free room in New York was,
and bought my ticket.

My first day in New York was three days before
my 23rd birthday. The weekend I arrived, I remember
feeling so overwhelmed by the amount of stuff to
do in *Time Out New York* and so intimidated by all
the many, many people walking on the street, all I
could do was stare out the window and contemplate

the possibilities. My birthday that year was very lonely. I tried to invite people out on the weekend before, but it was too last minute; besides I didn't know the hot spots to go to. I cutely called the man I was seeing, who for all intents and purposes was my boyfriend in college (but we couldn't call it that). He declined, citing another engagement, but said, "Thanks for thinking of me." On my actual birthday I had my second dreadful day at *New York* magazine and came home to an empty room. My friend's mother was thoughtful and bought me a slice of chocolate cake from the local Food Emporium. I sang "Happy Birthday" to myself while watching *Family Guy*. At least I had cable.

New York magazine was a place in its beginnings where literary greats like Tom Wolfe wrote stories that graced the pages. It was known for irreverence, catering to the wealthy elite of New York and their most pressing issues. I didn't know that when I accepted an internship there.

I arrived at *New York* magazine fresh and bright eyed, ready to partake in editorial meetings, write small items, and be fawned over, similar to how I had been treated at *Upscale* Magazine. And, hey, I had an Ivy League degree! I walked in, still with Georgia red clay on my shoes, and said, "Good morning!" to everyone I saw. I was all smiles, waiting for that red carpet to roll out, for someone to say, "Hey, how ya doing?" Silence.

Confused looks. I actually think I got a few scowls in response to a smile. I wasn't in Georgia anymore.

At *New York*, no one spoke, and I'm not sure it was personal. They barely spoke to each other, much less the new intern. I came with a blank slate, thinking that these were normal people — until I heard the woman next to me on the phone with her dad, saying, "If you can't park your Jaguar on the street, then just put it in a garage!" The guy next to me, a pint-sized guy with lots of energy, sent me on an errand to pick up his Mac book from his apartment. I go into the courtyard of a castle in the middle of New York, and later realize his mother was an extremely famous author. I was in over my head; somehow I had made it into this elitist bastion, and I tried to make the most of it. Every day my only tasks were to hand out office faxes and open mail. Oh no no, not with my degree! An industrious worker bee, I quickly started sending out office-wide emails, asking for work. My first assignment came from Jaguar girl. She wanted me to find gay couples in New York for an article she was doing on gay marriage. I searched and searched and came up with four black couples and two white couples. She came back to me and said, "Can you find someone who's...white?" Oh, of course. Having looked around, I should have realized that I was only one of two black women in the whole editorial department (and the other girl grimaced and frowned the hardest).

Soon I was busy. Doing LexisNexis searches for our public relations person (whose dad was a big political person in New York). Sorting through beauty products for a neurotic woman who only wrote articles about restaurant openings and new spa treatments. She also seemed to have an attraction to chemical peels and Botox. She would come up to me and mumble something like, "Find me the Oyster Club in Connecticut." Just one sentence. No instruction. But I found it because she wasn't repeating herself. At *New York* I was able to find what Paris Hilton was wearing on the front row of any given fashion show. I wasn't given her cell phone number; I had to find a way to find out. If you're placed in a river with no paddle, eventually you learn to swim to get to shore. And at that magazine I learned how to find things with little or no help, with zero guidance. It also taught me to do things, however uncomfortable, for the sake of a story.

While in the elevator bank one day, I cheerily said hello to an older man. Surprisingly, he warmed to my friendliness and we eventually started chitchatting. I told him I was the new intern, and said that if he ever needed anything, he could ask me. And the next day, ask he did. He started off giving me mundane tasks. Print out every article this famous author has ever written. Find the contact person for this city official. But then one day he told me he was working on a story and asked whether I would be interested in helping. I gleefully said yes.

This author, Dave Wattsman, was working on a story on New York firefighters' families affected by September 11th. My internship was back in 2004, so the wounds of that fateful day were still fresh. Dave was writing a story on how firefighters' wives were dealing with grief and the loss of their husbands in this national tragedy. Touchy stuff. But he got me, the new green intern, to help him report. My task? Call up the families of these firefighters and see if their families were willing to talk. Ask them how they felt, how their lives were. My first assignment was my hardest.

I had a list of about 20 names and had to look online at the Yellow Pages to find their numbers. Calling was hell. I'd get someone on the phone and tell them I was calling from *New York* magazine. Then I'd mention their son's name, and it was grief and tears, if not angry silence. I hated bothering them, I hated calling, but I learned that a bit of discomfort goes hand in hand with investigative journalism. The next week Dave invited me to Staten Island with him to the homes of many of the deceased firefighters. There I was, notebook in hand, making house calls to several families, sitting and watching as brothers, mothers, wives, cried over their loved ones. I felt like an invader. And when the story came out, guess what? It was a tabloid-like display on how firefighters' wives were living the high life, buying indulgently and spending insurance money profusely to mask their pain. How they took to drinking and dating the deceased's close friends to feel better. It was so disrespectful. But it was a scintillating, interesting story. Oh, and I received no reporting credit for that story. All those soul-jarring phone calls were unacknowledged. But when you're a scrub, you're just happy to be there.

Not all tasks were that difficult. I was sent to NYU to ask students about a peer who had recently committed suicide. Down at NYU, it seemed students barely knew each other. One man who lived in the bodega across the street from the suicide location didn't even know someone had just died; gotta love New York. While sniffing out a story from tragedy was the bulk of my work experience at *New York* magazine, the true lessons of the industry came from the people who worked there.

There was one other black girl at *New York* magazine; her beat was shopping and beauty. During my first week, I sensed we could be friends. She randomly gifted me a cashmere scarf and gloves (which I still own), a Roberto Cavalli silk robe, and other swag that she received from advertisers. I thought maybe we could be friendly. But as the weeks wore on, it became obvious that her initial generosity was an anomaly. For the rest of my time, Naja didn't speak to me. She didn't look at me. She didn't say, "How are you?" Nothing.

You would think that as the only two women of color in a publication, there would be some lunchtime commiserating or some sort of mentorship. She was just not interested.

Funnily, one day I was sitting at another intern's desk for the day, and she had left her email open. I couldn't resist, and allowed my eyes to skim over an email she had sent to a fellow coworker. From their short conversation, I could tell they were both Jewish, and that one had invited the other to some sort of event, maybe a Shabbat dinner. Their tone was playful and fun — they were buddies. It also probably wasn't a coincidence that this intern was getting published almost weekly, while I was still performing menial tasks. Not to say I was a stellar intern. That I was not. I had no idea what I was doing at *New York* magazine. My only prior experience had been at a black magazine with a staff of 12. I couldn't be invisible there, and people actually asked for my opinions and ideas. At *New York*, we were just sat down and told to grovel for work. At the time, I didn't know about pitching. I barely read the magazine! But still, there was no one there to tell me what I was supposed to be doing. No instruction. Nothing.

As time passed, I could kinda tell that I was not getting a job offer from *New York* magazine, as I had with *Upscale*. I was literally just taking up space, doing small tasks and going for coffee runs. I busied myself with freelance articles to make some extra cash.

While I was there, *New York* magazine was acquired by the father of one of my Harvard classmates: Ven Shanowitz. One day, while sitting at my desk, I overheard an editor make a case for a new hire, saying, "This kid is fresh out of college. He's talented, he just needs a job." After doing a bit of research, I found out he was referring to another guy Dan, who was friends with Ven Shanowitz in college. Dan also lived in my house at Harvard. I was familiar with him, but didn't know him well. Within a few days, Dan came in for a job and got it!

Here I was groveling for months on minimum wage, handing out faxes and opening mail with the same exact degree Dan had. But while allowances were made for Dan, who was "just a kid out of school who needed a job," I was passed over and scowled at. I was to move on to other jobs while Dan held his position as a reporter at *New York* magazine for several years.

After leaving *New York* magazine, I got in touch with Ven Shanowitz, who sent my information over to an editor at the magazine. Suddenly this same editor who had scowled at me in the hallways was eager to talk to me. Hey, politics.

When I was a student at Harvard, hearing about how the portrayal of people of color was unbalanced and negative, I thought I could be the one to change that. I launched into the publishing industry, not knowing just how cold it was to people of color and how unfair hiring practices were. *New York* magazine showed me that the world of media is a cruel, nepotistic place.

After *New York*, I found my first full-time job as a fact checker at *So Nice* magazine. I'll be honest: I wasn't familiar with *So Nice* and didn't really know what a fact checker was! But after I saw that I was going to be making a regular salary of $40,000 a year, plus benefits and vacation, all I could say was, "When do I start?"

Not So Nice; The Birth
of Fashion Bomb Daily

S O NICE WAS a new magazine. It focused on home, advice, and making life easier. I entered the halls of *So Nice* elated to have a full-time job with a regular salary and weekends. My boss at the time mentioned that office politics didn't exist and that people were generally pretty nice. What I learned was that any organization where human beings are involved has politics. Anywhere you work, you have to understand the pecking order: who is at the top and who is at the bottom. And if you are on the bottom, you have to finesse your way to the top. In most creative fields, it's generally not about how well you perform or how talented you are. We're simply humans, and typically, the person who gets the furthest is the person who is the most popular.

That person, for me, was Vanessa Nelson.

Vanessa Nelson went to Vassar. Brown-skinned and bubbly, she had a raucous sense of humor. She was loud, carefree, and ambitious.

Vanessa and I started at *So Nice* around the same time, and we were fast friends. Both young, black, and interested in publishing, we hit things off immediately. Our first few months at *So Nice* saw Vanessa and I, along with Ryla, a young braided creative in the art department, and Rosie, a Dominican Bombshell in the photography department, going to lunch together, dipping into industry parties, and visiting each other's homes. Like a sorority, we made a silent pledge to get ahead together and to glide to the top as a group.

We spoke to each other in the hallways, formed our own email chain, and gossiped in the lunchroom. I couldn't believe my luck that I had found work friends who could actually be my real friends.

All was fine and dandy until Vanessa and I discovered we both wanted to be in the fashion department. Vanessa was bold, rambunctious, and funny, and had a way of making sure her voice was heard. She declared, emphatically, in front of anyone who would listen, "I have a passion for fashion!" And perhaps because she said it the loudest, most people came to see Vanessa as the only black fashionista allowed at *So Nice* magazine.

While I was a fact checker, calling subjects in the magazine to double-check the spelling of their names and the validity of their quotes, Vanessa was the assistant to our editor-in-chief. So even though she was doing less...crucial work for the magazine (her main tasks were to make appointments and direct calls), she had the ear of the woman in charge. And if anyone knew Vanessa wanted to work in fashion, no one knew that more than our editor-in-chief.

Therefore, when I decided that I wanted to write fashion and started poking around, my work colleagues were very resistant. Vanessa was the fashion girl, hello!

I scheduled a lunch meeting with Linda, a brilliant brown-haired editor of our fashion department. Over sandwiches in the cafeteria, she told me, "You won't like fashion. People in the industry are mean. They'll look you up and down and twist up their face. You don't want that." Undeterred, I asked her if I could perhaps pop in to a few fashion shows if no one else in the department was interested. She replied, "We generally give Vanessa any of our spare invites." I was quickly learning about both politics and perception. The fashion editors could get a bit further by buttering up the editor-in-chief by way of her assistant. And, let's not forget: There seemed to be room for only one black girl who loved fashion at the magazine.

So life went on. I pitched stories to the fashion department about fashion history and style. Because I was smart, a good fact checker, and spent a lot of time with people on the phone, I was suddenly charged with interviewing fashion industry insiders and providing their quotes for different stories. My favorites to interview included Tim Gunn, FIT's Valerie Steele, and Clinton Kelly and Stacy London from TLC's *What Not to Wear*. I became a better writer, someone the fashion department came to rely upon when the subject matter revolved around more than the best jeans to wear for the season. But even though I eventually came to become quite a prolific writer for *So Nice*, penning stories that would be among our highest read (I was behind one of our most popular articles: "What to Save on and What to Spend on in Your Wardrobe"), I was still in the fact-checking department.

There was nothing fabulous about being a fact checker. The department was full of very eccentric types. My boss was a transgendered man with a wife and two children. My co-worker Cynthia would regale us with tales of her sexual escapades and online dating. Elmyra, a mousy misanthrope, would be at work in her cubicle, but had somehow erected a sort-of curtain so that no one could disturb her. It was a dorky department full of nontraditional nerds. Though I was a huge dork, I knew I didn't belong there. I wanted to be in the fashion department.

In 2005, the opportunity presented itself: The fashion department was looking to hire an assistant editor. I threw my hat in the ring and excitedly sent my résumé over. I'll never forget the day the company-wide email was sent out, informing everyone that Vanessa had gotten the job (with an added "Isn't she so fabulous?"). I had become so used to being passed over and undervalued that I just sighed and kept my nose to the grindstone.

I appealed to my boss and our deputy editor during our yearly assessments. I consistently asked if I could move to the fashion department or if the magazine could create a new fashion researcher or writer position for me. The answer was always no.

My job wasn't totally against me. They did allow me to write to my heart's content and even attend a few run-throughs. But that was it.

If the answer was no from my magazine, I thought, *Why not see if I can go to other magazines?* I made an appointment with Human Resources to see what my options were.

I went up to HR with a binder full of my published articles. The woman I met with asked me if I had more diverse experience or had a website, and I said no. She recommended that I start freelancing for other publications. She also suggested I create an eponymous website where I could house my résumé, PDFs of my published articles, and a biography. At the time, websites were definitely not hot. Most people didn't have a .com. But I decided to give it a shot.

In 2006, I linked up with a web developer from Harvard. With her help, we launched ClaireSulmers. com, which still exists today. But when we finished uploading my resume and published articles, I felt that it looked boring and not befitting of all the fabulosity the Claire Sulmers name implies. When I expressed my frustration with the lackluster content of ClaireSulmers.com, my webmaster suggested I start a blog.

I was honestly worried about starting a blog. At the time, blogs existed, for sure, but most were snarky side jobs that were written anonymously. I had heard stories of several people getting fired from their jobs because of the information they wrote on their seemingly anonymous sites.

I also had to think of the subject. Because I loved to shop so much, I figured fashion would be appropriate. When things were good my friend Tanya always said they were TheBomb.com. So because of my friends and fashion, I named my website *TheFashionBomb. Blogspot.com.*

It started off slowly. I honestly didn't know what to write about! Some of my first posts just introduced myself, talked about me buying sweaters and returning them, and featured pictures of me trying stuff on in stores. I bought the Idiot's Guide to Blogging and mastered some elementary HTML. I studied up on it as much as possible, even taking a one-day class at the New School on the importance of Search Engine Optimization. I set up an email account and created cute business cards.

Meanwhile, I studied as much as I could about the industry. I purchased Kimora Lee Simmons's book *Fabulosity*, and inhaled it. She offered tips on how to dress, how to create relationships, and most importantly, how to function in the fashion industry. In one chapter, she recommended gate-crashing parties if you couldn't get in. I followed her every word to the letter.

Per HR's suggestion, I also began freelancing for several publications, including *Essence* magazine. In my research, I had uncovered some of the hottest blogs of the time, like *Young, Black, and Fabulous*, *Cake and Ice Cream*, and *Concrete Loop*. I pitched a piece about the best blogs of the moment, and the entertainment editor was on board.

I contacted the editors of each of those websites, and they were more than excited to get featured in a national magazine. Thus, I began creating relationships with them. It generally takes three months from inception to publication for a magazine. I suddenly had a connection to the most widely read black blogs in existence.

When the article went live, I contacted each editor, asking them for their mailing address so that I could send them a copy of the magazine. I also told them that I had a blog myself, and that they should check it out and shout me out if they liked any of my content.

I started *TheFashionBomb.Blogspot.com* in August 2006, and within a few weeks, New York Fashion Week was slated to begin. After years of begging, the fashion department gave me one show invitation, and I decided to make the most of it. I would go to Bryant Park, go to the show, then see what other shows I could slide into. When I wasn't at shows, networking and taking pictures, I'd photograph street style and film people at Bryant Park. I'd speak to everyone who sat beside me. I started to collect email addresses for everyone I met, and soon started sending out newsletters with my latest exploits.

One of the most anticipated shows during New York Fashion Week was Kimora Lee Simmons's show: Baby Phat. It was fun, glittery, and over the top, with a hip-hop soundtrack. Every celebrity and stylist in the African-American community populated the front row, and anyone who was anyone was in attendance.

I asked around, and of course Vanessa Nelson had been invited. Still naive to her competitive nature, I asked her if I could attend with her. She told me that the invites were admit one only. Dejected, but undeterred, I took Kimora's advice; I decided, if anything at all, I was going to her show. I'd figure out how to crash.

I went to the Roseland Ballroom with my work friend Karl. We drove up with butterflies in our stomachs and got out across the street. We couldn't be early because we knew we weren't on the list. We got a drink and waited things out.

Though the show was scheduled to start at 8 p.m., a crush of people arrived around 8:15. Karl and I got into the crowd and pushed forward to a table with a list. We both mumbled Vanessa's name, and just like that, we got in. We were so excited! We went to the bar and had a glass of champagne to toast to our success. I saw so many exciting people, from Nick Cannon to Serena Williams to La La Anthony. I grabbed my digital camera and had Karl take pictures of me with all of them.

After buzzing around, we found two empty seats and sat down for the show.

It was electric, and played all the most popular songs on the radio — loudly. I bumped up and down in my seat and sang right along, all the while guffawing with glee and giggling with Karl. (If you look on YouTube, you can still find the video there.) I was so excited that I had gotten into the show that I skipped the after party. (I wasn't invited anyway.) As soon as I got home, I wrote about the show, including my own exclusive pictures and video.

I sent emails to my top blogging friends, who hadn't been to the show. This was before bloggers were even at Fashion Week. Because I had the exclusive, *Young, Black, and Fabulous, Concrete Loop*, and many more linked to my content. And they sent their millions of followers to *The Fashion Bomb*. Boom.

After Fashion Week, I did some research on what women liked to do online, and it turned out most women liked to shop and look at celebrities. So slowly, but surely, I started to incorporate more celebrity content. I'd reference *Young, Black, and Fabulous* and see what was new and which celebrities were out and about. Then I'd use my research background to break down the best outfits for *The Fashion Bomb*.

I got my first Mail Bomb in 2006. Someone asked me where to find a pair of socks, seen in a random picture from a Google Image Search. But because I was a researcher, I was able to find it, and I emailed the person with my response.

Then, I suddenly started getting emails asking: What shoes are those that Beyoncé is wearing? What are those heels with the red bottoms? What are those bandage dresses that everyone wears? And I was able to supply those answers: (Christian Louboutin and Herve Leger. Back then most celebrities didn't go further than Saks to shop, thus making my job that much easier).

Though I was still working full time, I came up with a schedule. Every Monday, we would feature Street Style. Tuesday, Fashion News. Wednesday, Wild Card. Thursday, What to Wear. Friday, Reader Mail or Mail Bombs. Because I couldn't write during the day, I set aside time on evenings and on weekends to update the site or schedule posts.

A few months later, I had heard that Marc Jacobs and Louis Vuitton were having an event for his collaboration with Takashi Murakami at the Brooklyn Museum. I lived across the street from the Brooklyn Museum, and thought, *There is no way there is going to be a fashion event right by my house and I'm not there!*

I asked around and found out that a stylist I was familiar with was styling Mr. Murakami for the night. I swallowed my nerves and gave him a call. I said, "Hi... this is Claire from *The Fashion Bomb*. I heard there is a Marc Jacobs event today. Do you think I can attend to cover for my website?" The stylist responded, coldly, "I recommend that you get in touch with the press office of Louis Vuitton." He hung up the phone.

I wrung my hands and looked around. I saw a prom dress by Jessica McClintock hanging in my closet. Hearing Kimora's words ring in my head, I decided: I am going to that party.

I slipped on my dress and some expensive-looking vintage costume jewelry and walked across the street to the Brooklyn Museum. I was directed to a table, with people checking off names on a list. I mentioned that I was friends with the stylist who had rejected my request earlier (not a total lie). They found his name on the list, and I was in.

Guests were directed to a room with a bar and champagne, and I grabbed a glass. Champagne always managed to calm my nerves. Out of the corner of my eye, I spied Marc Jacobs himself. Armed with my digital camera, I walked up to him and asked for a picture. He nuzzled into my cheek and smiled.

I went picture crazy at that party. I snapped flix with Marc Jacobs and Takashi Murakami. Kanye West performed that night, and I took a picture with him. I saw Anna Wintour on the way out of the event. I was so tipsy off of champagne, I even gave her one of my cards.

I groggily woke up the next day and wrote my recap. I received dozens of comments, with people congratulating me on meeting Marc Jacobs. I'm not sure if my readers knew that I was sneaking into all these parties. And of course I didn't tell them. But I knew I needed that access, caché, and exclusive content to drive readership. So I did what I had to do.

In between glittering events, I interviewed industry insiders on how they broke into the industry. I provided magazine scans of editorials featuring women of color. Diversity still wasn't embraced in magazines like *Vogue*, so *Fashion Bomb* became the place where we celebrated the strides of people of color in fashion. Our focus was on the African-American and "other" demographic that wasn't highlighted in traditional media.

Though I had lots of page views, comments, and exclusive content, I still wasn't having an easy time breaking into the fashion industry. Therefore, I similarly crashed shows at the next Fashion Week. Aside from the Baby Phat show, Sean John was showing at Cipriani's. I'll be honest, I don't even know how I got into that one, but somehow I got past the velvet rope and into a seat.

I busied myself doing "the Claire" — taking pictures with everyone important in the room, from Trey Songz to Cassie. I believe my friend Karl and I crashed together, again. (It's always nice to have a crashing buddy.) Karl and I sat down next to an editor for *Teen Vogue*. I chatted him up and got his contact info. I emailed him my web address, and he discovered the picture of Marc Jacobs and me. Within a few weeks, I was featured as *Teen Vogue*'s Blogger of the Moment.

I was getting lots of great press around that time. Aside from being linked to by my favorite blogs and websites, I was written up in *WWD*, *Essence*, and more. It got to the point where it was getting uncomfortable to come to work.

My coworkers at *So Nice* congratulated me on my *Teen Vogue* article. I was doing interviews with other outlets while I was at work. I sensed my boss was hovering, wondering what exactly I was doing. I would use my lunch break to scan magazines. I started blogging from work to keep up with everything that was going on.

Because I still couldn't get access to shows, I decided to ask for invitations to shows from my magazine email address, but made it very clear to everyone that I was asking for invitations to cover for my blog. Imagine my horror when I went to sit down for a show, and the whole *So Nice* fashion department came in to sit next to me!

Meanwhile, my work colleague Vanessa Nelson was not happy. She and her friends had decided to launch an online magazine called *Candy Drop*, but it never took off.

Rankled by my success, she told her boss and the fashion editor that I was using *So Nice's* name to get invitations to these events. The fashion director called my office phone, yelling, saying, "Vanessa says that she's not getting seats at shows because you're getting invites on our behalf! You can't do that!" I was floored. I wasn't used to anyone screaming at me aside from my mother! I calmly explained, "I have a blog. It's called *The Fashion Bomb*. It's very popular. Every time I get show invites, it's because of my blog. I don't know what you're talking about." The fashion director backed down, but I realized that I couldn't continue the way I was going for much longer.

I was also blown away by Vanessa. Wasn't she happy enough she had gotten the coveted position in the fashion department? Why would she throw me under the bus and try to get me in trouble?

In addition to workplace nonsense, I hated sneaking away from work to go to shows, or committing my lunch hour to writing. I resented having to do the boring day-to-day work that I needed to do to pay my rent. I hated having to hide the fact that I was writing at work...or minimizing all the fabulous things I was doing and the new people I was meeting. My time was running low and I knew that I'd eventually need to leave.

My first step was to apply to low-level positions at fashion magazines. I applied to be a copy editor at *Marie Claire*. I didn't get a call back. I sent my résumé for an editorial assistant position at *People Style Watch*. Nothing. I requested an informational interview at Condé Nast. The coordinator responded that they only wanted to meet with candidates they had an interest in hiring eventually. I never heard' no' so many times consecutively in my life.

Over the weekend, I would go for runs in Prospect Park. After a run one day, I cooled down on the grass. I stared at the sky and asked, "What's wrong with me?" I felt I was smart enough. I had great experience at a magazine that was well respected. I had a blog that was really popular. Why was that not enough to work in fashion?

Every morning, I would see planes fly by as the alarm sounded for me to go to work. I always wondered where those planes were going, and why I couldn't hop on a plane myself.

I was fluent in French and had a degree in the language that I hadn't used. It had always been a dream of mine to move to Paris for an extended amount of time. So I set my sights on Paris.

I found a large picture of the Eiffel Tower and made it my screensaver on my work and home computers. I told everyone within earshot that I wanted to move to Paris. In fashion magazines, it is common knowledge that one must start as an intern, then become an editorial assistant, then so on and so on. So I thought, *I can start at the bottom as an intern at a fashion magazine in Paris, and justify the demotion by learning French.*

I started to put out feelers. One of my fashion idols was Andre Leon Talley. After reading his autobiography I learned that he was bureau chief of the Paris bureau of *Women's Wear Daily*, the fashion periodical, at age 28. I looked up to Andre Leon Talley so much. He was Southern, black, obsessed with fashion, and had a degree in French from Brown! I just knew he would one day be my mentor, but handwritten letters and emails to him went without a response. If I couldn't get him to meet with me, I would at least follow in his footsteps.

I decided to email an editor at *WWD* in Paris about pursuing an internship. She told me that I needed a convention de stage to get an internship. When I asked her what that was, she told me, "I am not going to tell you the intricacies of what you need. Find out for yourself."

To say I was at the height of dejection would be an understatement, but life marched on. I had great friends and a boyfriend in New York City, so I reasoned that even if my job was depressing, I had a banging social life! It was one day at Habana Outpost over the summer that my friend's boyfriend asked me what ever happened to my Parisian dream.

I told him, "I haven't heard anything. It's too hard. It's almost impossible to find a job in Paris from New York." He replied, "You should just move there and see what happens." A light went off and I realized that no one was going to give me anything. I had to go for it and take it.

My father was a pilot for United Airlines, so I decided to fly to Paris a few weeks later and meet up with whoever I could. I connected with a freelancer for *People* magazine. I asked the editor at *WWD* if we could meet, to which she replied, "I see no use in meeting you if you don't have the proper paperwork." Can you believe people are so mean?!?

While I was in Paris, I linked up with an old friend from my days of visiting Paris as a teenager. At a café, over wine, I told him, "I want to move to Paris, but I just need a place to live." He said, "I think moving here would be good for you. My mom rents these 'tout petits' studios to students for 500 Euros a

month. Let me call her and ask her if one is available."
I waited excitedly as he called his mom on his small
mobile phone. After a brief conversation, he gave me
the details. He said, "My mom has a studio that's
available in October."

After our meeting, I took the line 1 to Place de
la Concorde, and got out at the big roundabout. The
sun was glinting off the top of the Obélisque, and I
sat down in front of the Tuileries and took in all the
passing cars. I almost cried from the sheer beauty of
it all, and knew at that moment that I didn't want to
be a tourist. I wanted to live in Paris.

As soon as I got back to New York, I put in my
two weeks notice.

❧ 4 ❧

From New York to Paris

TO SAY THAT my parents were unsupportive of my move to Paris would be an understatement. You would think that after my storied history with Paris, they would have at least given me the benefit of the doubt. But no. My mother asked, "Why can't you wait a year?" "Why can't you find a job first?" "What about your credit cards?" My father made up several scenarios to make sense of it all. He conjectured that I had gotten fired from my job, and that's why I decided to leave so abruptly. When that was shot down, he thought that the friend who was renting me my apartment was trying to sleep with me. None of this was true, but all of this was used to scare me or question my judgment. I wasn't listening. I was going.

After it became clear that I wasn't backing down, my father conceded to help me. He came to my apartment in New York the day of our scheduled flight and sat down with a newspaper as I rushed around him, throwing things into boxes, plastic bags, and the like to try to get my apartment cleaned up for my subtenant. As he propped his feet up, he asked, "Claire, did you plan for this?" I hated to admit that I hadn't, but I couldn't let a lack of planning stop me from fulfilling a lifelong dream.

My dad ended up helping me ship a few boxes. We spent an extra night in New York and flew out the next day. As we were on standby, the chances of flying out didn't look good. After making it to Chicago, it looked like our connecting flight might not come through. As we deboarded, we looked at the monitor to see about our flight to Paris. We thought we would miss it, but it turns out the flight was delayed. We rushed to the gate to find that two first-class tickets were waiting for us. 1A and 1B. I took it as a sign.

My father's naysaying actually hadn't stopped. While I wanted to sit back and sip some free first-class champagne, he grimaced in his seat.

I must say that Dad helped me out, getting me a 30 Euro cell phone and a week's worth of groceries. As he packed up his small pilot's bag to return back to Atlanta, I started to cry like a little girl. He hugged me and said all would be OK. Then he reached into his pocket and handed me 20 Euros. "Be good, kid," he said.

At that point I knew I was on my own.

While I was sure I would be super busy while in Paris, my first few weeks were in fact very lonely. I went from having a job, friends, and a neighborhood and city I was familiar with to absolutely nothing. I spent my days walking the streets of Paris, taking in the beautiful architecture. I took my journals and wrote in them while sitting in cafés, ordering the cheapest menu items available: omelettes and café au laits.

When I wasn't walking the streets, I was at home, working on *Fashion Bomb Daily*. Instead of not having enough time to focus on the site, I had the most time in the world! I was up on all the news. The comments kept me engaged and made me feel tied back to home.

Meanwhile, I was still in hot pursuit of opportunities at *Women's Wear Daily*, *Vogue*, and the *International Herald Tribune*. I pasted the mastheads of the magazines on the wall behind my computer. I remember emailing an editor of the *International Herald Tribune* to no response. Then one day I found her number and got up the courage to call her. To my surprise, she picked up! I introduced myself to her and told her that I was interested in working for the paper. She told me to email her to follow up. I did. No answer.

Thankfully, after two months, I was able to find the one job I was the most qualified for: teaching English. I started in the new year, just as my bank account was hovering close to zero and I was wondering how I would pay the rent.

Before I moved to France, I read a book that encouraged me to write down what my greatest fears were surrounding my dream. In response to the question, "The absolute worst that could happen if I did what I wanted to do," I wrote, "If I move to Paris, I'm afraid I will have no way of paying my credit cards; potentially lose my apartment in NYC; not make any money; not afford to live there. I'm basically afraid I will be living in poverty/completely homeless if I move." And in response to "What are the temporary outcomes and benefits?" I wrote, "I could ruin my credit, which would suck. I could stress myself out running away from creditors. But I think I would be happy and the possibility of travel might make it all worth it."

Well I wasn't completely homeless. But my credit was shot. I had run out of savings and wouldn't be paid from my job for two weeks. My credit cards were up to the limit and my bank account was bouncing like a ball. But guess what? I was fine.

Rent was late, but thankfully I rented my tiny room from a friend, so it was no problem delaying payment. The gorilla on my back (called Bank of America) was charging me upwards of $70 for bouncing checks, but the payments were made.

A week prior, when I sensed I'd be bouncing a check, I panicked. I cried, I prayed, I groveled and cried some more. I tried to think of quick schemes to get cash. I was unsuccessful. No golden parachute, no sign from the heavens, no reprieve.

But when I calmed down, I realized that although debt is not cute at all, it's not death. I was alive, healthy, smart, and beautiful. I would be able to pay the bank back in a couple week's time with my first payment from my job. I would be able to pay my rent at the end of the month. In sum, my worst fears came to fruition, but somehow it wasn't so bad.

Fear can paralyze you from moving. Fear paralyzed me for years as I contemplated the complexities intrinsic to up and moving to a foreign country with no savings and $30,000 in debt. When I finally decided to say "fuck it" there were so many naysayers, including my parents who feared that I'd be shiftless and poverty stricken. My parents were somewhat right about the poverty part, but I learned how to live with less, stretch 60 Euros for a week, leave the party before the metro closed instead of taking a cab, politely decline dinner and make spaghetti with meat sauce at home. Being at negative was not ideal, but it wasn't the end of the world.

And as I walked around Paris, taking in all the free sights and sounds, marveling at all the gilded statues and impressive buildings, I realized how silly

I was to fear being without. If I could look back at the secure life I had in New York: the 10-6 job, the great apartment in a nice area of Brooklyn coupled with the sheer boredom I experienced every day and the pain I felt when consistently passed over for promotions, I'd trade it any day for the check-bouncing, credit-ruining beauty of Europe.

At the high school where I taught, the children looked at me with confused stares. "Why did you move to Paris?" Increasingly this question became even more difficult for me to answer myself. When I boarded the plane I thought that my pluck and ambition mixed with Paris's stereotypical appreciation for all things American would equal a red carpet cakewalk to the fashion magazine of my dreams. But five months into the new chapter of my life I was still the average, not the exception. I was teaching English in a Parisian suburb two hours away two days a week. Living in a shitty apartment whose ceiling looked as if it would crumble and crack any minute. My clothes were last-last-last season. Shoes worn down. Bank account steadily hovering just above zero. I was ready for a change.

Before I was faced with this sink-or-swim predicament, I was a little less aggressive about getting my way. But now that I was facing a future of glorified babysitting, I realized that it was time to get serious.

I sharpened my teeth at Paris Fashion Week.

The paparazzi lights, photographers, and high heels of fashionistas barreled into town. I hadn't prepared, yet knew I needed to go. My burgeoning website was still blooming and readers knew I was in Paris. I couldn't let it seem as if I was as much of an outsider as I was. In New York I was schmoozing with stars and sipping champagne with the glitteratti. I couldn't come to Paris and just look on from outside the gilded gates! Besides, Fashion Week was also about networking. I had to meet and greet, do what I could to find a contact who could help me make my next career move. I had to go.

The rule in fashion was "it's not what you know but who you know." For some reason I was still following that rule, even when all of my calls and emails prefaced with "referenced by so and so" went unreturned. Still naive, I thought I could use a connection to hold my hand over the Parisian fashion threshold.

The first person who sprang to mind was my "mentor," an award-winning black fashion editor who was polite enough to respond to my emails and also grab a quick coffee when her schedule permitted. I'd been keeping her updated on my progress in France, so didn't feel awkward sending her a bright, cheery email as the collections started, hoping she'd like to meet up. I received an out-of-office response leaving her phone number. I gulped, got on Skype, and dialed.

I totally had practiced what I would recite to her voicemail, and wasn't expecting her to pick up on the first ring. But she did. The conversation went a little like this:

"Hi this is Claire Sulmers, how are you?"

"(*nervously*), Good, and you?"

"I'm great, wait...do you remember me?"

"No, I'm sorry, you'll have to remind me."

"Oh, I used to work at *So Nice*; I recently moved to Paris."

"Oh Claire, I'm sorry, I didn't recognize the last name! How's it going?"

"Well, I realized that you would be in Paris, and wanted to see if we could meet up since I'm here."

"Well I just flew in and I don't know what the schedule is like...I'm also on deadline so I can't think straight. Can you send me an email?"

"Sure, no problem."

"And how are things by the way?"

"Great."

As soon as we hung up I felt a flurry in my heart. I didn't hesitate to send her an email, apologizing for bothering her on deadline, but also taking the time to ask her if I could go to shows in her place. As a busy fashion editor, she was most likely invited to every show on the schedule: a seven-day onslaught of eight shows or more a day plus parties. No one could handle such a taxing crush, and I hoped to be her sub.

As I pressed send I almost felt relieved. Fine, she didn't remember me at first, but she perked up when

I jogged her memory. I knew this woman, or so I thought, and hoped she'd take pity on me.

She never responded.

As the shows started, I became anxious. Now going to the shows seemed an utter life-changing necessity. Kanye would be there! Models would be there! Everyone would be there but me, and that just wouldn't do. I didn't know how the system worked and was scared. Scared to show up without an invitation. Scared to be looked over and up and down. Scared of being carted away by security.

The week started, and still no word from my mentor. I tried another friend — a Midwestern girl I'd had a few drinks with during my short time in Paris. She started off like me, with nothing, and was now managing a French/English top fashion magazine. I asked her for unused invites and she said she'd see, but then there was a deafening silence from her end. No help. Nope, none at all.

As a last resort, I phoned a friend of a friend who I knew worked in fashion. I'd met him once at a drunken bottle-popping night on the Champs Elysees and learned that going to shows was his thing. He picked up and seemed to not only know who I was but sense what I needed.

"Hi Sene, this is Claire, Mike's friend."

"Hi, how are you? "

"I'm good, I know it's Fashion Week…"

"Listen, meet me at 4 p.m. by Colette, we'll go to a show."

I couldn't believe my luck.

Here I was, making uncomfortable phone calls and offering to tag along with a somewhat mentor or sort-of friend, when I was one quick phone call away from my first Parisian fashion experience.

"OK, meet you there."

I looked at the show schedule and realized it was the show of a designer with a cult-like following, Rick Owens. I literally jumped for joy and picked my first outfit.

I met Sene at Colette with his two friends, a model and a gritty-looking California guy. Turned out my friend Sene, a slick Senegalese man with a slight build, worked as a buyer for a huge Japanese department store. If anyone had a carte blanche to shows, he did. On our walk over to the Palais de Beaux Arts, we chit chatted as I excitedly thanked him for bringing me along. He smiled knowingly and I immediately felt at ease.

At the show we flew past security and made our way into the small room with limited seating. So happy to be there, I took my place and stood up against the back wall. I spied my mentor bright and shining in the front row, and mulled over whether or not I should go up and talk to her. After a bit of hesitation, I walked up and sat next to her.

"Hi, how are you?"

"Hi! How are you?"

"Great, how are things going?"

"Well I always am happy I still have a job. How are things with you?"

"The same, but it's a bit difficult to get papers to work here and things like that."

"That's so unfortunate."

As we yammered on a cameraman came and took our picture. He surely had never seen two black women sit on the front row and had to capture the moment. Blinking the light out of my eyes, I continued.

"Well I'm still working on my blog and on a book that I'd love your help on."

"Anything that demystifies the fashion industry is a great piece of work."

As we chatted, a PR person came and told me to move. I was clearly in the wrong seat. I got up and said goodbye.

"Great seeing you."

"Yes. Enjoy the show!"

And that was that. I didn't have the guts to ask her face-to-face to go to shows in her place. I thought an email would do. But not so. I walked back to my standing spot against the wall and took in the show. I fell in love and knew that that couldn't be my last show of the season.

After, Sene and I went to grab drinks by the Louvre. Black like me, he really seemed to sense the racism of the industry.

"Yeah, every time I go into a show, they look at me funny and ask what I'm doing here."

"I can only imagine. Thanks so much for inviting me."

"It's fine. Tomorrow I'll take you to a whole day of shows starting at 9 a.m."

"Oh my gosh you're such an angel!"

"I'm not an angel," Sene insisted, but I was convinced otherwise. Someone willing to help me for no reason at all was equivalent to a saint in my book.

Sene and I made plans to meet up later that night for a fashion party, and I met him at 11 on the dot to go into club Magnifique. We made a grand entrance and immediately sat at a VIP table. Apparently Sene was a regular there. He asked me what I wanted to drink and I ordered champagne while he sprung for a bottle of vodka. *A girl could get used to this*, I thought to myself.

Soon, personalities and publicists I recognized from New York filtered in. There was Marc C, the transvestite socialite who had scored a recent *Elle Paris* cover. Maria from Smash PR. It was like a reunion! We partied, danced, poured generous servings of Grey Goose, and Sene got more and more affectionate. First a hand around the shoulder, then a kiss on the cheek.

A kiss on the forehead, then an attempt for the mouth. I was tipsy but still had my wits about me, and Sene was *so* not my type. I'd dated so many guys before — white guys, black guys, athletes, swimmers — enough to know that I was not attracted to Sene in the least.

He seemed cool with my gentle rejection and kept the liquor flowing until the DJ played his final set. As we left, Sene tried one more time to go for the goodies. I politely declined. Finally, he asked, "Do you want to come to my place or I can come to your place?" I said, "No I'm tired, I'm going to go home." He asked again, but I declined, jumped into a cab, and told Sene I'd meet him the next day at 9 a.m. He looked disappointed, but nodded in approval.

I set my hair and alarm for the following morning and took a quick shower before picking out my liquid leggings and tunic. As I was steaming my coat, I received a text from Sene. "Claire, no shows this morning, will call at 1 p.m." A little let down but still excited about the big, full day of shows, I took a catnap until 12:30 when I received another text from my newfound friend, "Do you want to go to Comme des Garcons or Anne Demeulemeester?" I was suddenly super hype! Asking to choose between Comme des Garcons and Anne Demeulemeester was like asking to choose between $1 million or $2 million. Either one was just fine, and both were better than zero. I quickly texted him back my preference, and found the schedule online which revealed the show would take place a few hours later at 5 p.m. While I waited, I grabbed a quick sandwich but didn't feel safe straying too far from my apartment. I ate my meal in my home, on call, waiting for Sene to signal. Around 4:30, I sent Sene a message. 'Where should I meet you?' I innocently inquired. He responded, "I have another show for you." He told me to go to an address in the 6th for a show that I was sure the schedule indicated happened the day before. I smelled a rat. The show he mentioned wasn't happening that day, but I wanted to believe that he was telling me the truth.

I blocked my whole day out to hang with him and he finally gave me the location for a show I wasn't sure was happening. Still, I got dressed and made my way to the venue. I told myself that if he was indeed playing me for a fool, I'd straight gate-crash the next show on the schedule, Jean Paul Gaultier. I scribbled down the address and metro stop for the Gaultier show, and left my apartment feeling anxious.

I got off in the 6th arrondissement and walked past children and teenagers on my way to the venue Sene indicated. I knew something was funny, as I didn't see anything at all resembling a fashion show. No photographers. No women teetering in heels. No modelesque women handing out magazines. No lines. I bumped into a security guard not far from the entrance and asked him, with a sinking feeling, if there was a show.

He responded, "There was a show yesterday, not today." Sene had me fooled. And I was pissed.

I walked away, dejected, and sat on a bleacher. I stared at the sky, wondering why Sene had kept me hanging around all day. Why he lied to me. Sure, I wouldn't sleep with him, but was that all that stood between me and the fashion show circuit? More important, what should I do? The coward in me wanted to go back to my studio and snuggle into my familiar twin bed. But the fighter in me was pissed and wouldn't take no for an answer. I decided to pick myself up and try my hand at Gaultier.

As I walked to the train, I called Sene and told him the show wasn't happening. He acted confused, then was apologetic. "Oh, I guess I was confused." Yeah, confused about many things. Confused to think that I was the one to fuck with. And misled in thinking he could shit on me and it not have any consequences. I hung up and silently gave him the middle finger. I was determined never to deal with his trifling ass again. Or sleep my way to the top. Moreso, I was determined to go to the show with or without him.

I hopped back on the train and headed toward the Marais. I didn't have a plan for getting past the guards and crowds, just a strategy to feel things out and go from there. I arrived and could already see tons of people: fans hoping to catch a glimpse of a celebrity, photographers snaking around one corner, and the press line with two people in it. Damn, I was early. I knew the essence of acting like you were invited was to walk in with confidence, on time or late (never early), but I could gather that they weren't letting anyone in just yet. Between my nervous self and the front door were two young ladies and a tall, strongly built man with an earpiece and an iron clipboard holding the press list. I asked my fellow line hopeful if she knew what was going on. "I think we just wait here to get in." So I exhaled and tried to mask my nervousness.

Within 10 minutes, the Gaultier staff started to let the photographers filter in, and the press line was ever growing. An official-looking lady with blue eyeshadow and matching mascara asked loudly, "Why are they allowed in? What's going on?" As soon as she started inquiring the man with the master list received the signal to start checking off names from his press list. My moment had arrived. My palms were sweaty.

The woman at the very front of the line said her name and went in immediately. The woman right in front of me and next in line was petite and soft spoken, so the bouncer turned a bit and bent down as he listened for her credentials. As he knelt down, he tipped the list to the side slightly, and I was able to catch a glimpse of the name of a well-known New York editor on the list. I quickly memorized her name and the spelling. Within seconds it was my turn. I decided to use her name and see what happened.

"Yes?"

"Yes, I'm on the list."

"Yes?"

"Oh, I'm Katy Hollingsworth, with the *New York Tribune*."

I kept my voice low in case Katy Hollingsworth was in fact that woman with the blue makeup not far from me in line. But shit, he hadn't heard me.

"What? Last name."

"Hollingsworth?"

I asked instead of interjected. *This will never work*, I thought to myself.

"First name?"

"Katy."

"With the *New York Tribune*?"

"Yes."

"Do you have a press card?"

"No, I left it at home."

"Well, OK."

And just like that he lifted the velvet rope. I was in.

Once I glided past security it was almost like I was lost. I saw a large marble foyer. To the left, official-looking people. To the right, a staircase that led upstairs. I saw a group of people heading upstairs, so I followed them. When I reached the top, I had touched the promised land: the runway. It was bright and beautiful with red walls and a checkered black-and-white tiled floor. All looked majestic and larger than life. I was so happy. Though I'm sure Ms. Hollingsworth had a seat assignment, I played it cool, standing toward the back by the door while attendees filed in. I was one of the very first in the room, and tried my best to act like I was supposed to be there.

"Do you have a seating assignment?" one of the ushers in a blue striped sailor sweater asked me.

"No, I'm standing."

"Hmm, OK, well just sit here, and we'll tell you where to go shortly."

"Thanks."

I opened the program and started reading, shaking and hardly able to concentrate. I kept thinking that I'd get a tap on my shoulder any second from a burly-looking man who would cart me out by my fur collar. But no, I had breached the crucial threshold and everyone assumed I was supposed to be there. I breathed a sigh of relief and thanked GOD for his blessings. As I read my program, I caught my "mentor" out of the corner or my eye.

"Sheila, Hi!"

"Hi." She said curtly before finding her front row seat.

Her excitement from the other day was gone, and now she simply looked annoyed. I wondered if I had done something to her, but couldn't think of what. I had no choice but to think that maybe this black editor actually wasn't a mentor at all, but rather an old lady holding onto her title and front row seat by her stubby fingernails. I represented the new guard, the one who would soon eclipse her intellectual newspapers clippings with quick, funny, honest cyberblabber. If I were her I would've loved to be linked to someone like me, the only other black person in the room. But she didn't want to know me, and suddenly I understood that I was all alone. But then again I was so high from my coup I couldn't care.

More notables filtered in. I spied every big editor: Anna Wintour from *Vogue*, Carine Roitfeld of *Vogue Paris*, Anne Slowey from *Elle*, and Kate Betts from *TIME* magazine. (Yes, I knew them all by face and name). I was so overwhelmed. Though it was my time to shine I couldn't do anything but stare in awe and snap pictures for my next blog entry. *My readers will love this*, I thought, and I quickly got to work.

I found two well-dressed show goers and took a picture of them on the runway. Took pictures of the ambiance and got my video camera ready. I was in. Finally in. Of course I had to take pictures!

After everyone was seated, I found an empty chair and was excited to hear American accents. Feeling brave, I struck up a conversation with a cool-tempered Indian woman seated to my right. I saw on her chair that she worked for Bergdorf Goodman but didn't have it in me to ask her outright, so I played dumb.

"Hi, do you work for a magazine?"

"No, I work in retail. What about you?"

"I just moved to Paris. My goal is to work at *Vogue Paris*."

"Good for you; that takes courage. So how are you doing with your goal?"

"OK, but I guess I just got here. And I've emailed a friend of a friend over there with no response."

"Well, have you applied?"

I felt stupid. I hadn't. I had hoped my friend of a friend could get me in the door, but after four emails I was still empty handed.

"No, I haven't."

"Well, send a cover letter and résumé to the editor in chief expressing your interest. She should be able to help you."

"OK. Thanks."

Simple, yet poignant advice. I didn't know why I hadn't thought of that before. After the show, I went home and looked up my kind Indian sage. She was the head womenswear buyer for Bergdorf Goodman. She had to know what she was talking about.

The next day I started drafting letters to the editors in chief of *Vogue* and *Vogue Paris* along with the editors of *Elle* magazine and the bureau chief of *Women's Wear Daily*. I couldn't afford not to.

⟶➤●◄⟵

The story first appeared on the website *Jezebel.com*. White model Lara Stone had appeared in the October 2009 issue of *Vogue Paris* covered in brown paint. In one photo she wore a feathered headdress and matching gown. Needless to say, Americans, especially African-Americans, were *pissed*.

As the owner of an African-American centric website, of course I had to write about the story. I gave my readers a bit of history on blackface, and included why the history was so painful and why *Vogue Paris*'s editorial was totally unacceptable in the modern era. It was one of the most highly commented articles that week. I later wrote about the controversy for AOL Black Voices, and the story received almost 500 comments. *Vogue Paris* was taking a beating from everyone from bloggers to CNN. Their response: no comment.

My buddy Alexander emailed me in the midst of the controversy to see if I had written about it. He said, "Are you hearing about the scandal caused by French *Vogue*'s use of blackface? I expect you to write something about it on your blog...so irresponsible." Having already written about the issue, I responded haughtily, "I'm really sad you don't read my blog: (32 comments! Add yours)" He shot back, "How does this issue affect you?" To be honest, I was really disgusted with the French *Vogue* girls, whom I had idolized and admired for ages. I said, "I suddenly became very disenchanted with the whole idea of working for them. I realized the industry is made up of the SAME type of person, and that some of those people are frighteningly unaware and ignorant. It left a bad taste in my mouth." Then Alexander responded with a golden idea, "With this big backlash, it could open doors for you at *Vogue Paris*. Especially if you contact Carine Roitfeld again...I'm sure they'll be scrambling for a black writer/editor assistant to calm over things like, 'Look, we have a top black girl working for us, it's OK, we're not racist.' That's usually how things go... you know... I can see a smart, well-positioned letter from you stating you're a Harvard grad with a lot of experience in fashion and how you could be an integral part of her team, also reflecting the diversity of our society and its fashion culture, etc. Something to do right now while it's hot on the presses."

Thank GOD for smart friends.

After our exchange, I made it a priority to write the editor in chief, Carine Roitfeld a letter. I put it on my dry erase board and within days, I had a draft. I started it saying, "As an African-American studies concentrator at Harvard University, I watched the movie *Bamboozled* by Spike Lee about the unfair depiction of black people in the media. After seeing the film, I decided my role would be to diversify the staffs of major magazines, lending my unique culture and point of view to the organization." I went on to call the *Vogue Paris* team homogenous, their Lara Stone editorial racist, and to tell them that I would be the one to fix their problem.

My written French was horrible, so I needed a friend to proofread. I sent it to my American friend Chloe, whose French was better than mine, but she was sick and couldn't get the letter back to me quickly enough. Then I thought, *I know French people who could proofread.* First I sent it to my landlord, but he didn't reply within hours and I was impatient. So I decided to send it to my perfectly bilingual friend Guillaume. I said, "I wrote a letter to Carine Roitfeld of *Vogue Paris* about the blackface controversy and need help with grammar. I'd like to send it out *today.* Can you help me proofread? Please, please, please, please. It's attached. Say yes." Within hours he called me and gave me the lowdown on my Spike Lee, race-laced letter.

He said, "In France we decided the word race does not exist and we can't use that word. Then you mention Spike Lee, someone who is seen as a very militant person. With your letter as is, she'll just think you're crazy and never want to meet you. It also seems like you don't know French culture. You can't send this." We chit chatted and he gave me ideas of what to say to appeal to her. I thanked him for his edits and got to work on another draft.

The new letter said, "I've been in Paris for a year, learning the culture and people. Now I feel at ease to write to you. I feel that your Lara Stone editorial was misunderstood. I can offer you something interesting: my interest in fashion, my American culture, and my background as an African-American in Paris. "

On October 20th, exactly one year and a day after I moved to Paris, I mailed Carine the letter. I went to my favorite copy place on Rue du Fossé St. Jacques, and, as I had before, printed out the letter and my résumé on good paper and mailed it to 56 rue du Faubourg St. Honoré, where the offices of *Vogue Paris* are located. Then, two days letter, I sent Carine the letter via email. Within two hours, I got a response.

Her assistant Marie Laure said, "Dear Claire, thank you for your CV and your very interesting letter. I showed them both to Carine, and she would be happy to meet you in her office. When are you available?"

I literally almost hit the floor. I had been trying and trying for what seemed like forever to get a job in fashion, preferably at *Vogue Paris*. I was still staring at the masthead, right behind my computer so I could see their names every day. I also had my goals written right beside the masthead, with one that said, "I will do everything in my power—networking, emailing, and communicating — to be on staff at French *Vogue* by age 28." When I had the hope of working for *WWD*, I crossed out French *Vogue* and wrote in *Women's Wear*

Daily, but my goals were always intact: work for the best, now.

Finally, I had my opportunity — and I was terrified. It meant something to me that these fabulous people wanted to meet with me. It meant I had something interesting that perhaps could work for them. And while Condé Nast was shutting down foreign bureaus and laying off people at American *Vogue*, it seemed I still might have a chance in Paris. At this point, I would do anything for them. I would intern, I would assist, I would get coffee. I needed that name on my résumé.

As the days approached to my interview on October 27, 2009, I had flashes of insecurity. I was a lot bigger than all the girls at *Vogue Paris*. Also, I had dreadlocks. I was so different, but maybe that's what they wanted.

I started to doubt myself, and I knew I needed to stop. I was meeting with the editor in chief of *Vogue Paris* to discuss job possibilities. I needed to be fabulous and prepared. In short, I needed to make it happen.

The day of the interview, I put on my new Zara outfit and slipped on my stockings. I decided to go all the way with my makeup, and popped on a bright red lip. I let my curled hair unfurl, and looked at myself in the mirror — I looked pretty. And for a visual woman like Carine, I knew it would win her over.

I hopped on the train and listened to gospel on the way over. Kirk Franklin sang, "My God is an awesome

God…" I closed my eyes in the affirmative and prayed for the best as I stepped onto the Champs Elysees. The Elysees building on 56 Rue du Faubourg St. Honoré wasn't as daunting as it had been when I passed by a year prior. I walked through the wrought iron gate and stepped into the building. I told the receptionist, self-importantly, "I'm here to see Carine Roitfeld." Unfazed, she said, "Floor 6." There was surprisingly little security, and I slid on the elevator and checked myself out in the mirrors. All was in place; I was ready.

I came into the unassuming *Vogue* office and was literally blown away by how quaint it was. I was expecting bright white hallways, and a cushy setup. Instead it was a regular office building, with a very mousy French girl sitting at the receptionist desk.

I walked up and excitedly said, "I'm here to see Carine Roitfeld." She seemed unimpressed and quickly called Carine's assistant. When she got off the phone, she directed me to take a seat. Of course as I sat I started to sweat, so I fanned myself with my clips and résumé. After a short wait, Carine's assistant walked up. She was wearing a casual striped sweater, baggy jeans and flats! I was so surprised. American press made it seem as if everyone in the *Vogue Paris* offices were skinny and beautiful and wore heels. Her assistant was cute, yes, but a model she was not. I was immediately relieved.

I was escorted back to Carine's office, where she sat behind a large glass table. She was wearing eyeglasses that made her eyes appear huge. She seemed motherly and a lot less intimidating than she looked in all of her street style pictures. She greeted me warmly, and commented on my red lipstick, saying, "*Quelle belle sourire* (What a pretty smile)." We started off in English, and she said, "Tell me about yourself."

I gave her my clips and she started fanning through them. She said, "This is not what we do at *Vogue*," and I said, "I know, but I'm a fast learner." Then we spoke a little French, and then she called her assistant Marie Laure in the room and said, "This is what we're going to do for Claire. We're going to see if she can be in the beauty department. And we're going to see if she can join the website as an intern." Marie Laure nodded her approval and I was off.

I walked down the Champs Elysees after that feeling absolutely thrilled. I was ready to get my shine.

5

The Nobody at Paris Vogue

THE FABLE OF Chicken Little has several different endings, but all the stories start the same. It begins with a chicken who thinks the sky is falling because she feels an acorn drop on her head. Chicken Little, a spry girl, goes off to tell the king and brings her friends along with her. In one ending, a fox eats Chicken Little and all of her friends. In another, the characters narrowly escape. The moral changes, but the story generally conveys that if you think something is going terribly wrong, take a moment to ponder without panicking. Maybe it's not as bad as originally thought.

In my case, the sky literally fell before me, as it were, at 3 a.m. one Parisian night. I had fallen asleep, as I have been known to do, with my contacts in and makeup on, while watching a marathon online of my new favorite show *30 Rock*. I was nursing a hangover, so a good night's sleep and veg time were all I needed, but something woke me up and told me to finally get ready for bed.

I walked into my bathroom, whose ceiling had been leaking since my second week in the apartment. This damaged ceiling was a handful. At one point all of my makeup and toiletries were overrun with water. A large water heater, once placed over my toilet, had to be removed for fear it would fall on my head. This bathroom was shitty, but still it served its purpose. I made my way to the sink to wash the day off my face.

I heard something drop, and looked up to see tiny pebbles falling from a crack in the plaster. I peered as I saw more and more pebbles and debris fall from above. Instead of finish my nightly ritual, I decided to step out of the bathroom to watch what happened. Within minutes, right before my eyes, a thunderous, loud cloud of debris, concrete, and wood came tumbling down. The sky had fallen. I was petrified.

I immediately got out my camera and began snapping pictures. I was too flustered to figure out how to explain what just happened in French and knew a picture spoke louder than words. Not wanting to wake up my landlord in the wee hours, I sent him an email saying, "THE CEILING JUST FELL. OH MY GOD. I DON'T KNOW WHAT TO DO," with the pictures attached. I immediately told any and all friends who would be awake, then, stunned, walked back to the bathroom door to inspect the damage.

I stared in wonder at a huge piece of concrete on the floor and tried to pick it up. It wouldn't budge. This heavy slab of concrete could have fallen on my groggy head had I stayed in the bathroom two minutes longer. I would have been seriously injured if not dead. I was lucky.

After scrawling a note to my upstairs neighbors warning them to be careful of falling through their bathroom floor, I tried to sleep until morning. Only in the calm after the storm did the worried thoughts start to come in. *Where would I live? I didn't even have enough money to pay rent, how could I find a new place or such a sweet deal? What was I going to do?* I was now panicked, but there was nothing I could do then.

My landlord called the next day at 10 a.m. I was still sleep deprived, yet alert. After we debriefed, he apologized for boarding me in a death trap. Thanks! But I still had no place to live.

I called my friend Chloe, who lived with two Irish girls. I asked her if I could crash on her couch until my situation improved, and she acquiesced.

The initial plan was for me to sleep on the couch, but there was absolutely no privacy in her living room. But then we walked around and found a bathroom that had a large tub in it, a sink, and a door! Chloe had two twin beds in her room, so we decided to put the trappings of one bed on top of the tub. We put a plank on top of the tub, put a mattress on top of that, and added sheets. I piled my belongings in there and it was actually quite comfortable, aside from the crick I got in my neck from being on an incline with the faucet.

I was still sleeping on that tub when I attended my first Chanel show. While waiting for my paper-work to come through for *Vogue Paris*, I had snagged a freelance gig for AOL Black Voices, but I believe the Chanel press agent just saw I worked for AOL. At any rate, a lovely invite with a polar bear and an ice cap decorated the front of the invite. My name was rendered in beautiful calligraphy inside.

To attend the show, I put on my best ensemble: A Mackage coat I had splurged on while in New York and some boots. Though my coat cost upwards of $600, it still looked very poor and pedestrian next to the glamorous furs and borrowed threads I saw attendees wearing at the show.

Inside the Grand Palais, it was ice cold. I sat behind two gay men, who greeted each other excitedly. I was alone, so felt no qualms about eavesdropping on their conversation. One said, "Yes, I'm working for *Svelte* magazine now," to which the other replied, "Congratulations. I love fashion, so much...but there is no money in it! I barely have enough to eat!" I looked at him knowingly, then looked around the room, down to the front row where the well-heeled glistened in their

Chanel bags, luxe furs, and Rolex watches. I thought to myself, *Someone in this room is making money from fashion.* And in my mind, I decided that I was going to find out who that person was and follow in their footsteps. I wasn't going to accept a life of penury with the occasional show invite to make me feel special. At that moment, all I wanted to do were two things: to make money and to matter.

After the show, I milled around as street style photographers looked at me, then looked the other way. (They never wanted to take my picture!) I returned to my bathroom/bedroom and put my invitation in a prominent place. The show was magical, and I caught video of Karl Lagerfeld, a fashion god. I was on cloud nine.

That was the last Chanel show I was ever invited to. Even though I now wear Chanel bags, how ironic that the only show I was invited to was when I was sleeping on a tub.

Meanwhile, getting the proper paperwork to work at *Vogue Paris* was not easy, but I was able to make it work, and I began at *Vogue Paris* at the beginning of the spring, eager to hit the ground running.

My boss for Vogue.fr was a 24-year-old blonde girl named Mireille Robert. Seemingly sweet, Mireille had an obsession with sparkly pieces by Manish Arora and classic ensembles by Vanessa Bruno. She was smart and managed to run the whole website by herself.

Because I was the only non-French native speaker in the office, I was given the task of finding "street looks" during the afternoon. I would spend the morning combing the internet for the Look du Jour or Look of the Day, then writing something about it. In the afternoon, I switched out of my heels and into sneakers, put a large camera around my neck, and got release papers for people to sign. I was on the street style beat for both *Glamour Paris* and *Vogue Paris*. For *Glamour*, I was supposed to find the everyday girl who would shop at Zara or les Galeries Lafayette. For *Vogue*, the young woman had to be dripping in designer labels, thin, beautiful, and preferably white.

I got my route down pat, starting at Place de la Madeleine, then meandering my way to the Marais, where I always found well-heeled women navigating the cobblestone streets. Then from the Marais, I'd walk toward Avenue Montaigne, a street full of designer stores like Dior, Céline, and Chanel. Though I'd find mostly tourists, quite a few Parisians used Avenue Montaigne as their stomping grounds. I probably looked like a beggar, walking up to them in my frumpy clothes and sneakers, holding out an image release form that clearly said *Vogue Paris* at the top. In my American-accented French, I would say, "I'm a photographer for *Vogue Paris*, and I'm here photographing street style. I think you're very well dressed. May I take your picture?" I got a lot of "yes," but I also got a lot of "no." French people, I learned, are not about flaunting their wealth. Unlike Americans, flaunting wealth is seen as extremely vulgar. I remember wanting to write a story about the favorite things of rich French socialites and not receiving responses to my emails. The French are very subtle in their swag. But the job gave me tough skin. I was able to get up the courage to walk up to just about anyone and talk to them, and by the same token, when I didn't get what I wanted, I was able to shrug my shoulders and keep going. Rejection is a part of life, and many times you'll hear no more than you'll hear yes. But as long as you get a few yeses you're golden.

My street style section was doing well. We had weekly meetings going over the most popular features of the site, and mine was consistently in the top five. I knew the secret: The street style subjects had to provide their email addresses on the photo release forms. So when the article went live, I would email all the subjects and encourage them to tell their friends, which they did. Boom, traffic.

After a couple weeks, the head of Condé Nast digital and the editor for Glamour.fr pulled me aside, asking to talk to me. They said, "You're really talented and we are familiar with your work. We feel like we can really use you, so if you have ideas, please don't be afraid to offer them." I had tons of ideas! I told them that we should do more celebrity interviews.

That the fabled editors of *Vogue Paris* the magazine should have columns. (Who wouldn't want to hear the day-to-day thoughts of Carine Roitfeld or Emmanuel Alt?) I thought they should add a video component. And that we should do a story on the top blogs in the world. I thought that I had carte blanche to be fully creative, so went about attempting to get things done.

They rallied behind me as I did research for the article on the best blogs in the world. Once it went live, it was a hit. For the next few weeks, it was the highest read article on the site (because the bloggers were so excited that they shared the piece with their readership. Duh).

Encouraged by my coup, I reached out to a video crew, who said they would be willing to produce video for free. I reached out to socialites and celebrities for interviews. I even got my friend to coordinate an interview with Serena Williams, just as she was coming to town for the French Open. The head of Condé Nast digital seemed to like my ideas and even proofread my Serena Williams interview — twice. But when the Serena interview was set to go live, I asked Mireille, the editor of *Vogue.fr*, if we could press publish. Silence.

It seems she had a problem with it. And with me. Though I was bringing clicks and page views, she was not having it.

One day she called me into the lunchroom to talk to me. Agitated, she said, "I am the editor of *Vogue.fr*,

OK? Everything you do should go through me! You're here sending emails to everyone using bad French. You can't do that!" Not used to anyone talking to me that way, I responded calmly, "Jacques told me that I could do that. I sent all the emails through him." She huffed, "Well, I am the editor. You have to understand the hierarchy here." Then she turned and stomped out.

Just like at *So Nice*, I was dealing with competition. Mireille was younger than me and honestly didn't really know what she was doing with the site. Serena was a top tennis player who loved France and even spoke French! She had an apartment in Paris. At the time, *Vogue Paris* would have been the first *Vogue* to publish her. (American *Vogue* ended up putting her on a cover years later, and Anna Wintour always sits front row at Serena's collections for HSN.) But it didn't matter. Mireille was not a visionary, she loved to stick with the status quo. She wouldn't publish the interview because it would make me look good and potentially make her look bad. Here was an American intern who not only couldn't speak French as well as her, but was dominating her at her own game. And she couldn't take it.

And just like that, all my suggestions went to the wayside. My grand ideas to add some great elements to *Vogue Paris* were overlooked and buried. I went back to doing what I did at the very beginning: the Look of the Day and my daily street style.

Paris Men's Fashion Week barreled around the corner. The team met to see how they would cover it. I offered to take street style. Then Mireille piped up in the meeting, "We should do a story about the different types of people who come to Fashion Week! The fabulous editors who sit front row. The second-tier writers who sit in the second row. The assistants who are in standing room. And then the street style photographers and the nobodies who stand outside." The insult was there. Mireille was calling me a "nobody" — to my face! Everyone laughed at the concept of the "nobodies," so I grinned along, calling her a bitch in my head.

I was given the assignment of taking street style at the Louis Vuitton Men's show. I perched outside with the other "nobodies" and saw Jacques, the editor of Condé Nast digital, walk by me, nonchalantly laughing with his friends and barely acknowledging my presence. I guess he could acknowledge me in the office, but in the streets, he was too cool. Besides, I was a nobody! I shrugged it off and kept to my job. Then I looked up and saw a big SUV pull up. Pharrell Williams stepped out of the car, and photographers swarmed him. He emerged in a burst of color and bling. I had a huge crush on Pharrell and was smitten. I was too slow to get him before he disappeared through the door.

After Pharrell's grand entrance, it seems the show started. I looked up and saw some of my photographer friends going through the front gate that was formerly heavily guarded by security. Apparently after everyone was seated and the show began, the security found no reason to keep everyone out. One photographer slipped through and then we all bum-rushed the door and got in just in time to see the show end. In my mind, I thought, *I've got to meet Pharrell.*

I was in flats, so I hopped over a few benches and saw him headed toward backstage. I made a beeline for him and just as I got close, I poised my iPhone and asked, "Pharrell, can I get a twitpic for *Vogue Paris*?" He turned around, smiled, then said, "Beautiful skin." I beamed with joy, then happily sent the twitpic to the *Vogue Paris* team to add to our Twitter page. It was a huge coup!

I ended up hanging out afterward and was able to chat and take a picture with Pharrell. I told him about my website. He introduced me to Ronnie Newhouse of the Newhouse family (who own Condé Nast, and *Vogue* and *Vanity Fair* by extension). Unflappable, I gave her my pink business card. She told me, "Good luck." My life was made. I was on a cloud as I walked back to the *Vogue Paris* offices.

But as I made my triumphant strut through the door, I was greeted with silence. No one congratulated me or acted like it was a big deal. It was back to business as usual.

Meanwhile, my living situation had thankfully improved. One of Chloe's roommates, Nancy, found a new apartment, and for a few months I was able to sleep in her bedroom, equipped with a full-sized mattress. Then, a golden opportunity presented itself: A friend of mine from Harvard had another friend who was coming to Paris for the summer. A wealthy black socialite, she had secured a luxurious apartment in the 1st arrondissement, but unfortunately, her initial roommate was no longer able to come. With her parents scared for her well-being and wanting her to live with someone, they contacted me, and told me I could pay what I could to live in luxury. I went from a tub to a full-sized mattress to a fabulous apartment in the best part of town..

Though I was treated badly at my job, I had gotten to enjoy my time at *Vogue Paris* and my time in Paris. I dreamed of sailing through the streets in a yellow Vespa, with fresh baguettes and wine tucked into a bag. I wanted to have my own beautiful apartment and to just have enough to live. I appealed to Jacques around three weeks prior to the end of my internship to see about the possibility of being hired full time.

It was hard to pin him down.

Meanwhile, Mireille was acting much nicer. Sensing my pending departure, she gave me much more freedom to do what I wanted. When I suggested actresses to include in our Look of the Day, she eventually said, "Claire, I trust what you're doing. I think you can handle it." Perhaps she realized that I wasn't staying and thus not taking her job, so she was a lot less hostile.

The end of my internship approached slowly. The day prior to my last day, I was finally able to get Jacques to meet with me. We left a little before everyone got to work and got a café. I said, "I'd really like to stay at *Vogue Paris* if possible or get an extension to my internship." He replied, "We have one position open as a social media manager. That person will control the Twitter and Facebook for our properties, but I think you'd get bored of that." I insisted, "No, I'd be happy to do that. And perhaps while I do that, I can still do other things." He shook his head, but told me that he would ask his boss if that would be a possibility. He never did.

My last day fell in the middle of the Haute Couture collections, so the staff was busy with show reviews and the like. I had confessed my love for Justin Bieber at one time during my internship, so an editor played the Biebs loudly as everyone passed around cake and soda. The night before, I had written wonderful handwritten letters to everyone and given a speech. I said, "Thank you for all you have taught me, I will carry these lessons with me forever." Mireille gifted me with a Marc Jacobs wallet and some perfume. After hugging everyone goodbye, I was off.

I returned to my luxury apartment, feeling dispirited. Big on visualization, I had written down "I will work full time at *Vogue Paris*" on a Post-it note on my bathroom mirror. But I had learned that sometimes you make plans and GOD laughs. Or that GOD has bigger plans for you.

That same month, I got my first big advertising payment from *Fashion Bomb Daily*: $5,000. It was a big upgrade from the 500 Euros a month I was making as an intern!

While I was working at *Vogue Paris*, I had made a list of things that I wanted: A Balenciaga bag. Christian Louboutin shoes. One of the first things I did was go to Rue Saint Honoré and buy my first pair of classic black Christian Louboutin pumps.

It was my last month in Paris, so I did a bit of sightseeing, then packed my bags to come back to the States.

When I landed back in Atlanta, I went about sending out résumés to *Vogue*, *Elle*, and *Harper's Bazaar*, as I had tended to do. I thought, *With my experience at Paris Vogue, I surely can get a job at American Vogue!*

I wrote Anna Wintour herself. Her assistant responded that I could happily meet with someone from Human Resources. As I read that email, I started to cry. I wanted to meet Anna!

I went down to my mom and started crying, telling her that Anna gave me the Heisman and sent me to

Human Resources. She yelled, "Why are you crying? What do you need that you don't already have?"

And she was right. The month prior I had made $5,000 from my ad network, and I was poised to make another $5,000 that month, which was way more than I had ever made in the past. I looked up and suddenly, I was doing really well. So well that I didn't need a job. I no longer needed validation from *Vogue* or anyone else. I could work for myself.

So, out of necessity, I officially owned my title of entrepreneur and business woman. I never looked back.

The picture that put me on the map. Smiling with Marc Jacobs at the Louis Vuitton x Takashi Murakami Exhibit. April, 2008.

The first time I met Kanye West. At the Louis Vuitton x Takashi Murakami Exhibit. April, 2008.

With Lala Anthony at the Baby Phat show. September, 2008.

With Serena Williams at the Baby Phat show. September, 2008.

Feeling Myself at the Baby Phat Show, February 2009.

One of my first posts from Paris. October 2008.

Triumphant at the Jean Paul Gaultier Show. March, 2009.

When the sky fell. May 2009.

My first Chanel show. March, 2010.

With Pharrell Williams outside the Louis Vuitton Men's Show.
June, 2010.

When my look changed, life changed. Twirling in an Alexander Wang dress and Givenchy sandals. May, 2013.

Interviewing Fabolous for Fashion Bomb TV. December, 2014.

Interviewing one of my fashion idols, Kimora Lee Simmons.
September, 2015.

Partying with Rihanna. September, 2015.

Facetiming with Sean Combs. October, 2015.

Announcement photo for my Brand Ambassadorship with Dominion Charter Jets. August, 2016.

Toyota Brand Ambassador Photo. November, 2015.

With Fashion Bomb Daily readers at Cocktails with Claire New York. May, 2016.

Greeting Fashion Bomb Daily readers at my first international Cocktails with Claire in Lagos, Nigeria. December, 2015.

❧ 6 ❧

The Business of Blogging

BEFORE CONSIDERING ADVERTISING or making any money from your blog, you must realize that the first step is to create great content. Content is king.

You create great content by serving a need or filling a niche that does not exist anywhere else. As the popular phrase goes, there are riches in niches.

Once you have great content, you have to find a way to expose that content to the world. Send out newsletters or have bigger websites link back to you, sending traffic your way. When I first started, I'd create mailing lists with the addresses of blogs that might enjoy my content. When I featured something that might be of interest, I'd email them, and sometimes they'd link back. With the advent of social media, you can grow your page by using the proper hashtags or getting shout outs from Instagram pages with larger followings.

Once people come to your website, make sure the site is easy to navigate. Strive for zero grammatical errors, proper spelling, and accurate information. Explore similar sites to see what they are doing. Don't copy, but be inspired. Understand what the industry standard is, and do something similar, with your own flair.

Fashion Bomb Daily excels because we cater to our readership. When readers write in, we do our best to answer their questions. We also pay attention to comments and to which celebrities our readers flock to. We perform analytics and see that our readers love Beyonce, Marjorie Harvey, Rihanna, and Draya Michele. So guess what? Most of our content focuses around them. But with writing, you have to make sure that your content doesn't feel stale, so you have to be open to including other people. The very minimum requirement for someone to be featured on Fashion Bomb Daily is for them to have great style. It's simple.

Exclusive content is also key. But not just any exclusive content! We want to have interviews and videos with people that are of interest to a large group of people. Getting exclusives can be difficult, but the payoff is grand.

When I first started blogging, I was the one of the few sites with access to Fashion Week. I was the only site that had video of the Baby Phat show. I crashed gates and risked my reputation to get next to Marc Jacobs and Kanye West. I did what I had to do to get the scoop. Now, we are probably one of the few sites that will feature a look by Sarah Jessica Parker, followed by a look by Gucci Mane. We cater to the people; we give them what's hot and also what they want.

If Sarah Jessica Parker, Beyonce, and Gucci Mane have millions of followers each, there is a large chance that a large percentage of their fans are also fans of their style. We cater to the people who follow the hottest stars in the industry regardless of race. This is how we have been able to carve out a niche and also how we've been able to thrive.

Because we have an attentive audience of urban millennials, brands that want to target them will approach us. We make the majority of our money from advertising.

Learning how to Monetize
Blame it on my lack of television or ungodly amount of free time while I was in Paris, but by 2010, my website was raking in a good amount of cash. I was selling links to British companies for $200 a pop, and throwing up three a week. I was finding a way to monetize my recommendations to my thousands of weekly visitors, and was bringing in a percentage of whatever they spent.

Advertising came about slowly. I remember the first ad I ever sold on Fashion Bomb Daily was for a shopping site. They paid me $900 for a sidebar ad for a month, but I shrugged it off as an anomaly and treated myself to a nice dinner.

By the time I moved to Paris, making money from my website became a necessity, so I studied up to see how I could make my baby into a cash cow.

I devoured articles on ProBlogger.net and searched the web, simply using the key words, "Make Money from Blogging." A young man named Yaro Starak seemingly broke it down the best. He divided his sidebar into small squares...125 x 125, 300 x 250, so on and so on. And he got advertisers to subscribe to a monthly service to be featured inside each box. At the time, I didn't know how to determine what to charge, but your customers will tell you. If you quote a price and it's beyond their budget, you won't hear back! But if it's something that's doable for most, you have a sale. By 2011, I was making several thousand dollars a month just from selling sidebar ads, sponsored posts, and links.

Back in 2011, it was also all about the Ad Network. My Ad Network was Gorilla Nation, and they promised me that they would make me a good amount of money. They didn't disappoint.

Gorilla Nation was the ad network to all the 'urban' blogs like Necole Bitchie, along with a few mainstream sites like Pink is the New Blog. They'd go to different companies, like Tide or Pantene and sell our sites as an aggregate. Though they received a 50% cut of whatever deal they closed, back in 2011, the deals were pretty sweet. My first big check was for $5,000; that amount doubled by the end of 2011. By 2012, my ad network checks were in the several thousand dollar range. That's in addition to what I was making by selling ads independently. In a matter of years, I was living comfortably, eating well, shopping, and buying most of the things on my wish list (though my wish list continued to grow and get more expensive!).

In addition to ad networks, there are affiliate links. When you post a celebrity look or a look for less, there is an opportunity to make a commission. Sites like Reward Style and Shopstyle are the best for this.

Social media, namely Instagram is also another platform that you can monetize.

If you're on Instagram, you've definitely seen celebrities flaunting everything from Flat Tummy tea to waist trainers. They're doing that because it pays.

The types of ads you post and the price of your Instagram ads depends on your taste level. If you want to have a curated feed and want your ads to look a certain type of way, you should and can demand a higher price. Fashion Bomb Daily has 1 million followers right now. According to an article in Marie Claire, that would merit us at least $5,000 a post, but such isn't the case when rival gossip sites with more followers charge $1,000 a post. Get in where you fit in and find a happy medium, just don't sell you or your platform short.

It is a good idea to put together a media kit that tells potential clients what your blog is about, demographic data (the age, location, and median income of your readers), along with your reach. Create yet another document with ad rates and break it down by medium. Have a set rate for a blog post, and another rate for Instagram and Facebook posts. If you want to target one particular brand, create a presentation just for them, and explain to them how you can work together.

Your rates should differ based on the type of client. I'm fine lowering our rates for beginning designers, as they might not have the same marketing budget as a corporation. Whatever you do, do not sell yourself short, whether in regards to advertising or life. If you must make a living, make it a good one.

Fashion Bomb Daily Now

On site advertising has declined with the rise of social media platforms like Instagram and Facebook, thus signaling the advent of the influencer. Influencers are tastemakers, stylists, and leaders who inspire others by their lifestyle.

Around 2012, when I was swimming in cash, I realized that a lot of my colleagues who posted their outfits incessantly were being pegged for great opportunities.

They were sitting front row at fashion shows and being flown to Morocco and Cabo for press jaunts.

As an internet personality, you have to notice the trends and go with it. You also have to be very self critical. If I saw bloggers making major bank by being the faces of their brands, then I was going to join in.

I started to do more style diaries during Fashion Week. I gave myself a makeover, and dyed my brown locs blond. I started to get my makeup done and invest in my clothing. Putting yourself out there is not easy. While I was smiling for the camera, I had people telling me I couldn't dress, that I was obese, and had man hands and man feet. People called me Johnny Bravo, and for years, seemingly threw their hands up in frustration at my lack of ability to dress for my body type. I was told to get a breast reduction, butt enhancement, and lipo. But even with the negativity, I kept putting my picture up. I swallowed deep as I pressed publish.

What I noticed was that eventually people started to like my style. A lot of times, with people, it's all about exposure. I've learned that by reporting on the hottest celebs. Rihanna, Beyonce, and the Kardashian's are deemed beautiful and enviable partly because of their talents, and partly because we just see them so darn much. We feel close to them, like we know them. Though most celebs are pretty much always put together, there are moments when they are not (though to their credit, they tend to kill it most times they come outside). That said, after a while of people seeing your picture, they become accustomed to you. They don't care what you have on, they just like you. And in this digital media age, it is possible for you, just like many reality stars, to simply expose yourself to an audience, over and over again. And then suddenly, in their minds, you can 'do no wrong.'

Because of me posting my picture frequently, I was being featured in Glamour and paid to do NFL campaigns that would be featured in Vogue magazine. Teen Vogue asked me about my beauty routine. Elle.com included me a rundown of other style bloggers. People Style Watch came calling, and I ended up modeling swimsuits for them, and having that story promoted on the Today Show.

In 2013, I got my first ambassadorship with Toyota and my first ambassadorship check. A light went on in my head; I was determined to get as many ambassadorships as I could handle. I got on my dry erase board and wrote down a list of ideal brands. The brands I targeted were simply the brands I used on a daily basis, the brands that I used anyway. Why not get paid to endorse them?

My list included Ciroc, Fiji Water, a private jet company, and a few beauty brands. Though not all panned out, many did. By 2015, I was an ambassador for Colgate, Dark and Lovely, Toyota, Ciroc, Palm

Breeze, Dominion Charter Jets, and Curel. Each of those deals netted me several thousand dollars each.

Though most times brands come to you as they already have someone in mind they want to work with, pitching yourself doesn't hurt, either. I'll go ahead and say that I love Net-a-Porter. It is my favorite site because it has authentic luxury goods, the customer service is fantastic, and if you're last minute (read me) you can get a fabulous outfit the same day! They stock Alaia, Fendi, Givenchy, Tom Ford, Balmain, the list goes on.

I have been shopping with them for years and never asking for anything in return. But one day someone from their marketing department got in touch with me, asking me to promote a new project. I had a TV appearance coming up, and had my eye on a very expensive blazer from their store. After sending an email describing what I was going to do, they offered to send me the item, and I became a brand ambassador.

Though Fashion Bomb enjoys millions of readers and viewers, the marketing executive undoubtedly saw just how much I shop at the store. Already being a brand fan and being willing to advocate for them without payment is a great step towards getting paid.

Also, know that many times, cash payments aren't necessary. I always look at opportunities as such: Is it going to service my bottom line or my image? If the answer is yes to either, I move forward.

When you have finished a campaign with a brand, it's not good enough to work with them just one time. You want to work with them for years and secure an ambassadorship check every year for consecutive years. So, do your best work. Interact with the people who hired you. Give them absolutely everything they want. Throw in a little extra. When you're done with the campaign, send them a summary of how everything worked out. Offer and give as much information as possible. Go over and above.

The industry is small and people talk. I once worked with a brand that gave me a nice sized check, which was great, but the people in charge of the brand were super annoying. Instead of allowing me to make something organic that would work the best with readers, they wanted me to participate in a glorified commercial. Not all brands get it, and they don't want your creativity to flow. That's ok when they are writing the checks; you also have the right of refusal! I'll be honest, I gave them attitude. I thought they were too demanding and out of touch. And they never worked with me again. Don't do this to yourself.

Be easy to work with, but also try to go out and find new opportunities. If a brand you want to work with is having an event, go. Show your face. Meet up with whoever is in charge of marketing. Smile. Get their card. Report on the event.

It doesn't always work out. I went to an event for a Chinese watch brand that was looking to expand into the US market. I loved the product and wore it all the time. I contacted their PR, going so far as to call the person in charge. They were slightly receptive for a bit, but decided to ultimately pass on having me as an ambassador. It happens.

If you want ambassadorships, it is going to be a constant search for new opportunities. Networking is key. Take time to have those dinners and lunches. A lot of times, brands will want to work with you because they like you and you meld with their brand identity. Go to parties with people, make time for coffee. There are humans behind every brand. Get to know them, and take a genuine interest in them.

Working for Free?

When I first started out, I did things for free all the time because I simply wanted the exposure. There is a moment and a time when it is appropriate to work for free. But after you have paid your dues, your time is money. You should get paid.

No matter how big or small, you should always ask if there is a budget. If the question is no, but you'd still like to do it, ask for something that would help make the situation easier: car service, or for them to cover your hair and makeup, for example. If they can't do that, then think: Do I want to do this? Would it make me feel good to extend myself? If the answer is yes, go for it.

A reader recently wrote in, asking me to come speak at her high school, to children who were under-performing and needed encouragement. I'm happy to do that.

It is important to give back to your community. When I was growing up, I didn't have mentors or anyone who really took time out of their day to come speak to me. Therefore, I am happy to be that person to someone else. Our community needs leaders and people who are in it for more than the money. I don't write for the money, I write because I am passionate about it. But I also realize that there is a time limit to what I am doing.

Perhaps 1 or 2 of the blogs I wrote about for Essence in 2006 are still around today. Trust me, there were times when the owners of those sites were on the cover of Black Enterprise, detailing how they made millions. With the fast pace of digital media, there might come a time when people don't want to visit your site anymore. There also may come a time when you simply don't want to keep up with the grind of writing every day, without vacations (I never take vacations!). As such, it is important to save your money. Use your influence and your skills to make money, and save it.

You never want to be a slave to trends, you want to do this so that you have a comfortable life for years to come. Invest and make your money grow.

Speaking Engagements

Another way to make money from blogging: become a public speaker. Most bloggers don't like to speak in front of crowds. We find comfort behind the warm glow of the computer screen. But while you're typing away, you don't realize that you are unwittingly becoming an expert in various fields. You're an expert in blogging, for one, but you're also a style expert, you have a perspective on being in a creative field, you have insight on being an entrepreneur. Go out and speak about it!

Speaking engagements are great for many reasons: you are typically speaking on panels with other accomplished people from various fields, so it's great for networking. If you speak in front of large crowds, there are invariably people who are not familiar with your work, so you gain new fans and followers. Lastly, speaking engagements pay! There are some speakers that make $10,000 an appearance. Do 10 talks a year, and you're in the money! Becoming a professional speaker takes time, and it doesn't matter how much you yap if you're not motivating or inspiring people. The goal when you speak is to have people clap and stand up because you're moving them in a certain way.

You can't motivate a crowd or get booked for more speaking gigs without being a good speaker. When it comes to speaking, practice makes perfect. But you can also consult with a professional.

Almost every time I speak in public, I go and see an acting coach. She offers feedback on my tone, how I'm moving, and also video tapes me so that I can see myself. I also saw a voice coach for a while, to help me practice my breathing. If you want to be good at something, practice and take lessons. There are unlimited resources available at your fingertips.

Everything from colleges to independent companies have budgets allocated for speakers. Get plugged into the speaker circuit and watch your money grow.

One of the downsides of being a creative and a freelancer is that you don't know when your next check is going to come. Thus, I've begun securing 50% payment for opportunities where I will have to travel or make time in my calendar. The 50% deposit is to secure my date, and I receive the balance at the conclusion of the event.

Events

Events are another great way to make income.

In 2013, I started an event called Cocktails with Claire, which is a networking party for readers. We traveled from New York to D.C. to Atlanta to LA, welcoming hundreds of readers at each stop. While it is a great opportunity for face time with readers (and a wonderful occasion for fashion enthusiasts to network with like minded people in their city), it is also an opportunity for brands to be physically placed in front of consumers.

Create a deck that outlines the opportunity. Tell them dates, the typical attendance, and what you can offer them. For Cocktails with Claire, we have sponsors, we have vendors, and we sell tickets.

Take A look at What You Consume

If you're making a lot of money and are not good with money, I'd highly recommend getting a financial advisor and a CPA/bookkeeper. If you don't have someone who can do that for you, find one. NOW. Taxes are not a joke, and you could look back after several years and realize you spent all your savings and tax money at Barney's.

My financial advisor made me go through an exercise to track my expenses (which everyone should do as an entrepreneur). I realized that I spent $5,000 a month one month on Ubers and $4,000 on food. That's $10,000 a month on food, drink, and transportation (I was using Uber X's!). Stop the financial bleeding by being aware of what you spend and then make efforts to cut back.

Once I saw how much I used Uber, I contacted their team to see if I could be an ambassador. I contacted

Grubhub and Seamless, two services I use to order food from home, to see if they had an ambassador program. I also partnered with Eat Clean Bro to receive free meals in exchange for promotion. Once you have a certain amount of influence, you should start angling to exchange your influence for free services..

If Grubhub and Seamless are not down for the cause, then take a look at which restaurants you frequent. Write about them and speak with the manager to see if people who follow you can come and get a free drink, for example. If the restaurant sees a serious spike in sales, of course they'll want to work for you.

Whatever you want in life is possible, you just have to take the steps to get it. We all start by doing something for free. I used to advertise for absolutely everything I did. But once brands and people started to see that I was generating revenue and business for them, things changed.

If you are a fashion blogger, you can eventually get free clothes. If you are a beauty blogger, you will receive free product. If you are a food blogger, free food. If you want free food, clothes, and makeup, launch a lifestyle site. Your influence is powerful.

⊱ 7 ⊰

Looking the Part

F
OR SOME REASON, it took me a while to realize that my look was holding me back.

By nature, I am somewhat conservative. I love a classic, preppy look: Think button-down shirts, blazers, and crisp jeans. Though it might work for some, in fashion, standing out will definitely get you far.

It can be hard to develop a singular look with a small budget, but thankfully you can find loads of options from Topshop, Zara, and smaller online boutiques. With lower-priced brands, look for simple pieces that can be easily mixed and matched. Try to avoid getting something boring. Of course you need the basics (white button-down, black pencil skirt, black blazer), but you work in fashion! Don't be afraid to be bold and trade in that black pencil skirt for a slinky metallic bottom or opt for a pink leather jacket over a navy blue. Study up on the color wheel to see which colors work together and also experiment to know which colors work best on you.

Some of my go-to colors include white, cherry red, bold blue, and blush pink. Don't be afraid to try new things. Also, take a good look at your body and analyze your best asset. What do you get the most compliments on? Show them off! A lot of people tell me I have nice legs, so 90% of the time, you'll find me in a dress or skirt, showing them off. I am top heavy, so V-necks and scoop necks are the most flattering. I don't have a donk or a rotund behind, so pants or skirts with volume are a sure bet for me.

If you are pretty clueless style wise, consult a friend or stylist. There are lots of stylists, but not every stylist is made equal. Try different stylists and ultimately stick to the one who gets you the most compliments. I once spoke to Patricia Field, the legendary stylist behind *Sex and the City*. She said the mark of a good stylist is when people come up to her clients and tell them they look beautiful.

So many people in the fashion, music, and entertainment industry are stylishly unaware. They don't get likes, and comments are tearing them to shreds. Confidence is great, but if people are constantly slamming your look, fire your stylist and get a new one! There are lots and lots of stylists out there, and if you're truly challenged, just go to a store and see if someone there can help you put together a look. Everywhere from J. Crew to Topshop has in-store stylists who can help you put something together.

The Evolution of Claire Sulmers

In fashion, you have to stand out. I adopted locs when I was in college and have come to love my hairstyle because it is relatively low maintenance.

I'll be honest. I tapped a couple image consultants when I was starting to become more prominent as the face of my brand. They had successfully styled an artist who was regularly featured in *Vogue*. They were expensive, but they were worth every penny.

Though box braids were hot at the time, they encouraged me to keep my locs, but to make them more distinctive by dying my hair blond. They also advised that I get my makeup done for public appearances. They wanted me to go in a Rick Owens direction, and suggested loads of sumptuous shoes, dresses, and jackets to wear. I followed their directions to the letter. Not everything worked, but it was definitely a direction. Though I no longer work with them, they did give me the suggestion to change my hair, which has become my signature.

I'm a girly girl, so I try to convey that by the way I dress. I love sequins, fur, skirts, high heels, and glamour. I'm luxurious, but relatable. You'll find me in anything from Balmain to Topshop.

I know which silhouettes work for me and I know what I like. But because I have to dress up so much, I've started to have a lot more fun with fashion. I'm not afraid to wear shocking pink or enter a room with a voluminous fur dragging on the ground. In fact, I wouldn't have it any other way!

Developing a signature is the easiest route to go when shopping. It helps you to filter through the hundreds of options and find something that is distinctly you.

Most people in fashion have a signature, whether it's Anna Wintour's bob and sunglasses, Andre Leon Talley's cape, Grace Coddington's bright red hair, or Carine Roitfeld's smoky eye and cinched waist. Before my transformation, a fashion friend suggested I adopt a signature, and I suggested I wear bright, bold lip colors. She encouraged me to keep thinking. Your signature should be something that speaks to your personality, but also offers a heightened sense of who you are.

How to Shop

My style is a mixture of high and low. I shop it up at Zara, Topshop, and the like, but tend to spend on shoes and bags and select classic items. I am a lover of shoes and have my share of Giuseppe Zanotti, Jimmy Choo, Givenchy, Casadei, Gianvito Rossi, and more. I also invest in bags. I have a black Givenchy bag, a gray Stella McCartney bag, and a metallic YSL bag that I wear with everything.

The great thing about investing in bags and shoes is that you can always get at least some of your money back if you sell them via consignment or eBay. Most clothing loses its value the minute you put it on your back, but if you buy a Balmain blazer, for example, you'll most likely get your money's worth and more. Invest in timeless pieces. Save on costume jewelry and trendy things.

If you can help it, don't buy retail! Before I could afford the latest and greatest, I familiarized myself with consignment shops that sell authentic luxury items for less. Though some look down their noses at Rent the Runway or Bag Borrow or Steal, a lot of times in fashion, you have to fake it until you make it! There is no shame in you borrowing a dress or bag and giving it back. When I first started going to Fashion Week, I would wield around Balenciaga, Louis Vuitton, and Miu Miu bags I got from Bag Borrow or Steal. I did that until I could afford to buy my own.

Consignment shops like A Second Chance Resale are also good places to troll for luxury items. I got my first Chanel bag for less than retail at A Second Chance, along with Hermes jewelry, belts, and more. Though it is certainly an experience to go to the Hermes store and yell, "Charge it," you don't always have to go the full-priced route, especially if you are trying to save.

No one else will know your Chanel is from a secondhand store.

Grooming

When I come to an event, everyone can expect me to have my makeup done, my hair done, and my nails done.

You don't have to spend a ton of money on makeup. Most makeup artists charge $150 a pop, but after going to a beauty conference, I found a young lady who will do it for $75 — and she does a great job.

My hairstylist charges me $30 for a style. Get a gel manicure for $40 and have it last for a few weeks.

In fashion, you simply have to be on point. The entire industry is about how you look and putting forth the best version of yourself. I've skipped out on parties because my hair wasn't done. One time, I was told that I'd need to go on camera for a pilot, and my makeup wasn't done. I found the nearest MAC store and got my makeup done + lashes for $50. Was it the best makeup ever? No! But it was something.

People in fashion love pretty things and, like magpies, are attracted to anything shiny. Give them something to ogle at.

Please know that yes — people will look you up and down with disdain. I remember seeing Andre Leon Talley at a show and him looking at my busted Christian Louboutin pumps in horror. When I used to work a *So Nice*, an editor informed me in the elevator that it was about time I threw my shoes away. I'm hard on shoes.

All that to say, be as polished as you can. Get your clothes dry cleaned. Don't wear anything stained. Get an iron or a steamer. Make sure your jewelry shines. Pay attention to those small details. They will get you far.

Work With Smaller Designers
Though we all love Stella McCartney and Missoni, there are loads of young designers looking for promotion. Hit them up and see if they can slide you a gown or an outfit for a dressy event.

I met a young designer from Brooklyn at a very small fashion show I hosted. She made me a dress based on eyeing my measurements, and it fit perfectly! Now, I call her every time I'm in a pinch, and she gives me the pieces for free because I promote her. There are lots and lots of young designers who would be willing to do the same if you just ask around.

Your Style
My life changed when my look changed. Suddenly I opened myself up to hosting and speaking opportunities; just like that I was asked to be on TV. Your look matters, so curate it wisely.

❧ 8 ❧

Not Everyone Wants
to See you Win

MY INTRODUCTION TO Lisa Turner started online. I had written a post about Beyonce wearing Thierry Mugler in Paris, and Lisa left a nasty comment, saying that Americans were stupid and didn't know anything about European fashion. She intimated that I had stolen the information from her. (I hadn't.) I deleted her comment and wrote her an email, requesting that she leave the site and never visit again. She didn't comply.

Over the years, *Fashion Bomb* became known as the site where you can find all the looks worn by black celebrities. Lisa's site was more general market, and she reaped the benefits. When *Vogue* featured the hottest bloggers of the day, she was one of the few people of color spotlighted in the feature. She was invited to all the shows and dressed by designers. Though she was an industry darling for quite a few years, she never seemed happy with her success, and always seemed to be looking over her laptop at what I was doing, and leaving nasty comments with each keystroke.

I'm not one to necessarily hold a grudge, so I shrugged off Lisa's wayward comment and decided to befriend her the first time I went to Milan for Fashion Week. I didn't know anyone in town, so I roomed with two girls who were friends with her. She was standoffish at first, but I'm a nice person! And she seemed impressed with the fact that I was staying up late to update my blog. Apparently she thought I was a regular slacker. Her initial problem with me is that she thought I stole her content, which was preposterous. While she got her rocks off detailing every look from the Cannes Film Festival, I was busy reporting on the BET Awards. I felt like what we were doing was like apples and oranges, but she saw me as competition and a threat.

While in Milan, we became friendly. She actually wasn't a terrible person, and seemed mildly sweet — even a little cheeky. We had breakfast and a few dinners together. I was the object of a local soccer player's affection, and she tagged along on a date with him and me. (I wasn't about to go on a date in a foreign country with a stranger.) I still have a picture of us posing, bright eyed and rosy cheeked after that dinner.

Milan was a notoriously difficult city for me to break into. My first season there, I barely had any invitations. Meanwhile, Lisa was invited to Gucci, Fendi, Prada, you name it. The fashion industry absolutely adored her. So after a few days of getting close to her, a mutual friend and I decided to tag along with her to shows.

I'll never forget, the first show was Fendi. We all got into a cab together, and I swear she was aware that neither I, nor our mutual friend, had invites. Still, we went. We all got out of the car, and Lisa breezed in with her invite. Our mutual friend, Heather, and I went to the press list. We knew her name was on the list, so we both used it and went in. We did the same for a couple other shows...Gucci and maybe one other. It was fun, it was a game and seemed totally harmless... that is until Heather told Lisa and all hell broke loose.

Lisa was not happy at all that we had used her name to get access to shows. She was incensed, and wrote me a long email expressing her disgust.

She typed:

"I hope you are well and enjoying Fashion Week.

I've recently received some very unsettling news.

Two PRs from different agencies have informed me that someone of your description had used my name to get into shows during Milan Fashion Week.

If this is true, I would like to kindly request that you do not do this in the future.

I was happy to share my invitations with you, but you have to remember that PRs know my face and there is at least one PR from the US, UK and Europe on the door.

This has put me in a really embarrassing situation and I've had to explain to them that you were working alone, which you were because I never gave you permission to use my name to get into shows.

I will instruct PRs that this is happening and that I do not endorse nor do I encourage this type of behaviour and I will ask them to not to leave my name at the door to prevent this happening in future, or next time I will check myself in with everyone with a clipboard.

Please be assured that I have not given your name nor your website to any of the PRs I have spoken to in relation to this, so it will not to ruin your chances for getting into shows for next season.

I hope you enjoy the rest of your fashion week."

I responded:

"Hi, understood. Heather indicated that you didn't want us to do so; I was somewhat under the impression at first that you were OK with it, but thanks for telling me you're not.

Hopefully now that I know my way around Milan I won't need to use any name but my own."

But she wouldn't accept an apology!

She typed:

"I don't understand where you got that impression, as I never gave it to you.

Please accept responsibility and don't push the blame back to me.

We are professional women and we should act accordingly. It's hard enough to get these people to respect us without acting like a gang of hood rats trying to gatecrash a show."

Did she just call me a "gate-crashing hood rat"? Yes, she did.

But I kept calm and responded:

"Hi, I am accepting responsibility. I don't ever want to fight with you (please know this), and appreciate the generosity you extended with invitations.

You didn't give me that impression or say implicitly or explicitly that it was OK. I received that impression from other people. I should have asked you instead of assuming you were fine with it. Now I know you're not fine with it, and I will respect that."

She didn't respond, and I thought it had ended there, but oh no! A few weeks later, an advertiser got in touch with me, saying that Lisa had maligned me in an email. When the advertiser asked Lisa if they could advertise on her site (i.e. give her money), she responded, *"I do not value those sites you have listed. Especially the Claire from Fashion Bomb Daily who spent the whole of Milan Fashion Week using my name to get into shows without my consent. Because she was too embarrassed to admit she travel all that way and only received one invite. I don't want to ever be associated with her site. Also I do not accept advertisers outside of my ad network."*

This bitch was crazy and out for blood.

I drafted an email to her asking why she would say that, but never sent it. I kept quiet, hoping she would simmer down and go away. She didn't. I could tell she was crazy from the way she was offering up unsolicited negative information to someone who couldn't have cared less about Milan or Fashion Week. Not too long after, I received word from a mutual friend that Lisa had gone ahead and emailed every publicist in her Rolodex, telling them that I was a gate crasher using her name to get into shows.

For my first season in Milan, I wasn't totally iced out, receiving invitations to Blumarine, Moschino, and a few others. But for my second season and many others in Milan, I didn't receive any invitations. This woman had managed to black-ball me in the industry.

It's hard enough being a black women in fashion. Lisa was black and German. Always looking to support my fellow sisters, I had written about her on Essence.

com and suggested her for a feature on *Vogue Italia*. They ended up doing a video interview about her. But while I was working to uplift her, she was working to tear me down and undermine all the hard work I had put into my site.

Even though *Fashion Bomb* continued to climb in traffic and social media numbers, it was the black sheep of the fashion industry. Requests for invitations were overlooked. Though we rarely see black bloggers on the front row, Lisa would have been one of the few black faces to populate a fashion show. And she wanted to be the only one. In an interview, she said that she dreamed of being like Pat McGrath or Edward Enninful, black people making waves in the industry. Friends would send me pictures of her smiling it up with Stella McCartney, backstage at her show.

One season, I saw her in New York at the BCBG show. She was sitting across the aisle from me. I texted my friend Tanya, who was familiar with our situation, and asked her what I should do. Religious and faithful, Tanya said, "Just kill her with kindness! Be graceful." I got up and said hello to her, and she mumbled a curt hello. It took all the grace of GOD not to retaliate against her, write her nasty emails, or even write about it on social media. She didn't extend the same courtesy. She alluded to our situation on Twitter and even wrote about it on her website, years after the initial incident.

I couldn't understand WHY she had such a problem with me. We were friendly. We went out to dinner. Yes, I used her name to get into a few shows, but was that so wrong? I learned about doing it from Kimora's book! I saw loads of my colleagues crashing shows left and right. Crashing shows was part of the form and function of Fashion Week. And at the end of the day, I was only doing it because I couldn't get in otherwise. My readers wanted and deserved that content just as much as anyone else!

But I kept quiet and cried to myself when I was passed over yet again for Fashion Week. I found a way to make up for my Fashion Week isolation. In Milan, in particular, I made friends with locals. I also learned that fashion shows aren't where the real networking happens: the parties are! So if I'd have a week in Milan with nothing to do, I'd go out every night and stay out until 5 a.m. I'd sleep in, then do it again the next day. I met some amazing designers and stylists partying in Milan. I managed to find the silver lining and, every season, prayed that next season would be different.

A few years later, Lisa wrote me to apologize. She typed:

"Firstly, I want to congratulate you on the new design and branding of your website.

I am writing because with Fashion Week just around the corner, I don't want to drag on the animosity between us any longer.

You can accept or reject my olive branch, I will leave that entirely up to you, but my intention is to assure you that I do not have any ill feeling towards you and I wish you continued success in the future."

Always ready to kill with kindness, I responded:

"Thank you so much for your email. I happily accept your olive branch.

I never had any ill feeling or animosity towards you, just admiration for your excellent work and work ethic.

I wish you continued success as well, and a Happy Fashion Month!"

She never responded. A couple years later, I learned via *People* magazine that she had decided to shut down her site. She wrote her last post just at the advent of awards season.

What she hadn't learned was how to evolve with the times. There was a moment in 2011/2012 when bloggers were making loads of cash from on-site advertising. But things had changed, and it was time for bloggers to be the face of their brands and also capitalize off of social media.

Lisa was socially awkward. She rarely took pictures. She couldn't really dress. It was likely that her site simply wasn't making enough money to sustain, and she was working too hard to do it by herself. And GOD don't like ugly.

Let me tell you, it KILLED me to stay quiet while I suffered. I read every Bible verse, while she sat there and initiated a smear campaign against me. And then, just like that, she was gone.

I wrote about her demise on my personal site, *The Bomb Life*. She wrote me an email about it. I didn't even read it. Heather, our mutual friend, found the post and wrote nasty comments, which I swiftly deleted. I was over her, over them, over her drama, and done with her antics. Besides, she was a non-factor.

A few lessons for those who want to play dirty in the fashion industry: The world is small and people talk. Lisa had gone about writing nasty things about me to everyone in her contact list, and I had actually seen her do that to other people. Electronic correspondences are forever (which is why I was able to copy and paste our conversations verbatim).

Rule #1: Never write a nasty note or email, because that stuff can be forwarded on and on for perpetuity.

Rule #2: Watch what you say. If she acted crazy to me, she acted crazy to someone else, and perhaps they were the wrong one.

Rule #3: Try not to step on toes, and know that karma is real and will come to bite you. You get what you give, so try to give only positivity.

Who knows if her site would still be up if she weren't so nasty? But I'm sure she got a reputation for being hard to work with and plain old mean. Who wants to deal with that?

She thought that her reign would last forever, but it didn't. And I am doing the tootsie roll, the Wobble, and the electric slide on the grave of her website. Ding, dong, the witch is gone.

The worst people can seem to prosper, and it seems unfair. But they won't prosper for long. Stay faithful, and do the right thing. Always.

9

Love and Business

EVERY BLACK WOMAN hears those statistics: black women are most likely to get passed over in online dating. We are undesirable. Marriage rates for black women are in the toilet.

I was determined not to be a statistic.

I knew I was cute from the scores of guys trying to holler every time I stepped outside. But while I was able to 'hook up' and go out on dates with ease, the committed relationship seemed just out of my grasp. Until I met TJ.

Calvin, a friend from Harvard who I knew nominally well, appeared out of the ether in 2014, looking to invest some resources into Fashion Bomb Daily. His proposal? To assist Fashion Bomb in 'scaling.' He said he was starting a new company that helped small businesses grow. I was intrigued. I didn't look too hard at his references because I knew him from

Harvard and took having a Harvard degree to mean that he was minimally competent. Word around town when we were in school was that his Dad was a super wealthy investment banker. His Facebook feed was littered with pictures of him with Bill and Hillary Clinton, or images of him in his Hamptons summer home. At one point, he was one of Harvard's most eligible bachelors. I could admit that I had found him attractive, but he had dated and slept with too many of my friends for us to ever date without stepping on toes (this happens frequently in majority white schools; not enough cute, slightly charismatic black men to go around). Now, he was married, with a wife who was interested in fashion. Not sensing any reason to keep my guard up, I agreed to meet him and his wife for drinks the following week.

His wife, Sarah, was gorgeous and tall with long black hair. She had a great body and could wear anything from hip hugging jeans and crop tops to pencil skirts and button downs with ease. A Southern belle, she had an eagerness and ease about her. She made you feel as if she cared about you and was invested in your happiness. It was over drinks when we began to discuss dating. She said, "Are you seeing anyone?' I lamented, "I'm as single as a dollar bill." Calvin and Sarah groaned together and said, "What's wrong? You're so beautiful, any man would be happy to have you!" I didn't know what was wrong. "Perhaps they're intimidated?" I conjectured. But then Sarah said, "You know what? I'm going to think. Calvin has lots of friends. I like to think of myself as a matchmaker," she grinned. Then she said, "You know what? Calvin is celebrating his 30th birthday party down in New Orleans in a couple weeks. There will be lots of single guys there. You should come!" I'm always one to take an adventure, and with my flying privileges, I could get down to NOLA at little to no cost. After following up with Sarah, I realized that a fun weekend in New Orleans with new, well connected friends would only be $300. I signed up.

Day one down in New Orleans was chill yet fun filled. Calvin had gone to Harvard Business School after graduating from undergrad, so the house was full to the brim with many brilliant people...but none that really caught my eye.. I shrugged, grabbed a drink, and dipped into the pool, simply happy to be enjoying a new experience. During the day things were cool, but at night, even more of Calvin's friends seemed to trickle in. That's when I met TJ.

A Harvard graduate as well, he looked mildly familiar, and I asked him how he was. His hair was crisply cut, and diamond studs glinted in his ear. He said, "I'm good!" The Harvard question to ask is always, "What are you up to these days?" He offered a vague answer about being involved in 'business' and that things were good. His answer was curt and he didn't seem to want to go into detail, and I didn't really care that much! So I smiled and went on my way.

Later that night, TJ circled back again for moonlight drinking and smoking with Calvin. I was still by the pool, but by this time was pretty tipsy, kicking it with new acquaintances. Calvin and TJ were sitting down, smoking, when I ambled up. They made some comments about my appearance, saying that I was looking good in my bikini, to which I muttered a thanks. Calvin said, "Yeah, Claire has been stuntin on them. All the guys in college used to have a crush on her." TJ countered, "I didn't have a crush on her, I wanted to fuck her." My mouth dropped open. While I should've been turned off, I was intrigued that someone would be so bold as to say that to me.

And thus our tryst began. We ended up hooking up that night. TJ got his wish. And then suddenly, we were inseparable. The next few days in New Orleans saw us dipping into bars, dancing in the streets, and going on ghost tours. While most of the guests on the trip packed their things up on Sunday, TJ and I decided to extend our stay. I could fly for free, and he seemed to have unlimited funds and a flexible schedule. We got a hotel in the French Quarter and laissez les bon temps rouler. We took shots of tequila in the middle of the day as I told him my dreams for unlimited riches and wealth. He hopped on his cell phone, showed me a picture of a pile of cash, and said, "I'm going to make love to you on that one day." A little tipsy, I joked, "Are you the devil?" He laughed and said, "Why'd you ask me that?" I shrugged it off as we took another shot.

That night found us strolling down Bourbon street, in search of Cajun food. We had drinks in our hand, and as I looked right, it seemed someone had knocked TJ's drink out of his grasp.. He was incensed, and walked back to the faux offender, asking him to buy him another drink. The guy looked startled and said, "No man, there must have been some mistake." But TJ wasn't hearing it. He proceeded to yell, "You're gonna buy me another drink." He then took his shirt off and got ready to fight.

I had never seen anything like this in my life. I didn't understand why TJ was so upset about a $5 drink--to the point he wanted to fight in the streets. Finally a bouncer came up, diffused the situation, got TJ a drink, and we were on our way. Being with TJ was exciting, but also outrageous, confusing, and scary.

After grabbing dinner at a hole in the wall, we walked down a side street. There, he said, "I've been asking GOD to find me someone who was equally yoked, and he sent me you. You are my soulmate." I felt like he was moving pretty fast, but I was flattered, so went with it. He went on to say, "My mom has AIDS. She is dying. Meeting someone like you has given me hope." I felt shocked yet honored he would share such personal details with me. I was locked in.

While TJ poured his heart out, someone passed by on the street and yelled, "Get a room!" He replied, agitated, "Don't do that, man! Don't do that! I'm having a serious moment here." He faced me and continued, "I thank GOD I found you," before we headed back to our hotel. I felt myself so lucky to have found someone so devoted so soon, that I happily skipped alongside him, not thinking his behavior was out of the ordinary.

We decided to leave the next day, and as soon as I hopped on the plane, he called me singing, "All I do is think of you…" By the time I reached New York, he had apparently lost his phone and called me from another number. He said, "Yeah, I lost my iphone somewhere in the airport. I have Delta looking into it." As we chatted from his new number, he booked a ticket to come see me in New York a few days later.

TJ and I moved quickly. We spent all of our time together, even though he lived in Detroit and I lived in New York. Because I could fly for free, I flew out to see him often, and he would come see me as well. We quickly became a couple. After only 6 weeks, he had already declared his love for me, and started talking marriage.

Though New York Fashion Week is generally the worst time to visit someone who works in Fashion, TJ insisted upon coming at that time.

The day before he came to town, he asked, 'Are you going to come pick me up from the airport?" With my busy schedule and the proliferation of yellow cabs at Laguardia airport, I said, "No, why not just take a taxi?" He replied, "You must not care about me if you can't come pick me up." Feeling guilt, I acquiesced. He had come to town with nothing to wear, so asked me if I could stop by Saks to get him an outfit. Of course I said no! But he made me feel bad and told me I was shirking my duties. One day, I had a ton of shows, and he called me nonstop. I obviously couldn't pick up the phone, but when I finally called him back, he said, "I don't think you're really ready for a relationship. So we can just be friends." Panicked that I would be losing out on a good man, I told him I would be more attentive. And thus my slacking began.

The Fashion Week TJ came to see me is the Fashion Week I quit freelancing for *Vogue Italia*. I had had a very rigorous job for *Vogue Italia* where I covered Fashion Week for them in New York, London, and Paris. The Italians didn't play! I typically covered 30 shows per city, and was required to turn in my show reviews within 3 hours of the end of each show. That Fashion Week, I skipped most of the shows, preferring to lay in bed with him. Finally, I wrote my editor at the time and told him I quit, and that I also wasn't going to be going to Europe to cover the shows. I was done. I wanted to live and love! I'll be honest, I probably needed a break, but no man should ever encourage you to be irresponsible. TJ didn't need to come during Fashion Week, he just wanted to go to the parties and pose with celebrities. I never worked for *Vogue Italia* again and haven't been to Europe for Fashion Week since that season.

At the time, I didn't care. I had a man who I would get married to. He talked about having babies and shared my vision for the white picket fence, the mansion, and the cars.

All of this seemed like a dream come true, coming from a woman who hadn't dated anyone seriously in quite some time. I thought I had finally found the one, and I was over the moon! But some things didn't sit well with me.

TJ always had large sums of cash. Sometimes $5,000 at one time, always in $20-$100 bills. It never made sense to me WHY he always had so much cash. Why not put it in the bank? I asked my friends and they were confused as well, some even saying that they didn't even have $5,000 to deduct from the bank. But I looked the other way.

He also always seemed to lose his phone or have a new phone number. At one point I had eight different phone numbers for him. He had conversations off to the side that I wasn't privy to. When I visited him, his apartment had little to no furniture. He spent all day on the corner with his friends.

I grew up in the suburbs and went to private school so I didn't know that all of these were clear signs that he was probably a drug dealer. I shrugged off my suspicions. I loved that he had two Rolexes and flossed cash (even though he never ever gave me any). I loved that he always flew first class. TJ, to me, had all the trappings of a somewhat perfect guy. He was brilliantly smart, good looking, and seemingly successful. He was a charmer, and had a bright smile and dimples to match. He told me he loved me, truly and deeply, and that GOD had put us together. But I never got a clear view on what his job was.

His story was that he owned a liquor distribution company called Liquor Lounge. But when I visited his 'office' one time when I went to Detroit, it had no computers and a broken toilet. One day, while out on the town, we ran into a few Harvard folks, who ended up inviting TJ and I to their house. He made a big show of the liquor he stocked for his company, and one of the men said that they had a contact at a huge distributor that could be helpful to him. But after that meeting, TJ never followed up.

When I visited him, we frequently stayed in hotels. Sometimes we'd stay in 3 different hotels over the course of several nights. One day, his Chief Executive Officer called him to say that a few cases of liquor had been stolen from his facility. He erupted in rage and yelled at her, sensing she was accusing him of having a hand in the theft. I had honestly never been privy to so much drama and stress in my life. Moving from space to space, losing phones, and getting into fights simply wasn't normal for me. But instead of run away, I felt sorry for him and tried to be there for him.

Meanwhile my friends and family were not on board. My mother was wary of him from the get go, but I couldn't understand why. One time when he was in New York, I coordinated a quick meet up at the airport. Apparently TJ hadn't covered the bill, and when my mom asked him what he did, he didn't provide a satisfactory answer. For that reason alone, my mother told me to be careful. She was never happy when I called her from Detroit. She encouraged me to write things down that seemed out of the ordinary. No matter how hard I tried, she didn't like him, and he started to be disrespectful when talking about her. I knew that talking about my mother crossed the line, but I was still under love's spell.

TJ hadn't had an easy life. His mother was addicted to heroine and the story was that she left him at a gas station when he was five years old. He went from foster care to foster care, getting into trouble as a young man. That was, until he met his Cousin Christina, a woman who saw lots of promise in him. She got him off the street and put him in good schools. She was so impactful in his life, that he excelled in magnet school and ended up going to Harvard. He was an American success story, and I was proud of him.

I knew he had scars from his childhood. That he was still in touch with his mother, who was now diagnosed with HIV, and was a recovering drug addict. I knew that he still had ties to 'the hood.' But I honestly thought he had left everything behind, and was looking to lead a better life.

TJ seemed dazzled by my lifestyle. A few weeks after we met, I was slated to attend the BET Hip Hop Awards, and he wanted to come with me. Normally with press events, I go solo because...it's a job. But no. TJ wanted me to apply for credentials for him. Eager to please, I did. He got to Atlanta too late to pick up his credentials, but he had the gift of gab. Somehow when we hit the press entrance, he was able to get past many layers of security just by talking. He stood amongst the press, somewhat in the back, and watched me as I took pictures with Teyana Taylor, Snoop Dogg, and many more. He just observed what I did before asking me to take a few pictures of him on the red carpet. He had gotten dressed with care, wearing a Versace jacket and crisp white pants. He took a few pictures, then posted to Facebook, with the caption, "Simply networking here at the BET Hip Hop Awards." He made no mention of me being there with him. He made it seem as if he had come on his own, as a result of his accomplishments. But he was my plus one.

TJ always wanted to be my plus one. Let's be honest: I go to lots of celebrity laced parties, award shows, and events. Though it looks like a party, it is work. I am usually there capturing content, taking pictures, and reporting on it for social media. He wanted to come and network for his own purposes. A red flag didn't go off in my head. I thought it was darling that he wanted to experience things with me. No red flags, until a planned press trip to Jamaica.

Press trips to the Caribbean are always part vacation, part work jaunt, so I was excited to bring my new boyfriend along for the ride. My photographer, Phil, and I left on Thursday, and had managed to get the Jamaica tourism board to get a ticket for TJ also, that left on Friday. We landed in Jamaica, and then I called him. No answer. I called the next day. No answer. The whole weekend, I was in a panic, calling his friends, emailing his work colleagues, and sending Facebook messages. No one had any information on his whereabouts. But then Monday came, and I turned on CNN to see TJ's mugshot on TV. He had been arrested for storing almost half a ton of marijuana in his house. TJ was no small town drug dealer. He was a Detroit Drug Lord. And he was incarcerated.

Him lying to me for the duration of our relationship about his vocation should have been a dealbreaker for me, but I was a hopeless romantic and an optimist. And I didn't want to be alone.

My parents told me to cut all ties with him and to not answer his calls, but I couldn't. I needed answers.

He showed up at my doorstep in New York City looking rough and gushing with apologies. He told me that he had been doing it all along and that he started dealing drugs in college because he couldn't afford to pay for his tuition on his own. He said he felt inferior to the rich kids at Harvard. He said that while he was in school, kids always thought he had rich parents because he always had a new car and new clothes. Little did they know that he was dealing cocaine as a side hustle.

He explained that he wanted to let it go after graduation, and found a few corporate jobs, but that those jobs couldn't deal with his personality. TJ was a bit of a know it all, but I came to find out that he was also a big liar. He had no morals or ethics and simply could not be trusted. He always thought that he should be bigger than he was. He wanted all the best in the world but he didn't want to work for it. He relied upon his brilliant brain to con the system, and most employers could see through that, thus he wasn't able to keep a job. So he turned back to the streets. I didn't know he was conning me because he was one of the best liars I had ever met.

After shedding more tears, TJ told me that he wanted to change and that he didn't want to continue doing the wrong thing. What could I say? I was in love. So I told him that he needed to move out of Detroit and come up to New York with me. I would give him a job at Fashion Bomb Daily. I would take care of his bills, I would feed him and make him feel at home. I would be his rock, his supporter during his court dates. Real Love knows no bounds, I thought. I was down for my man.

I knew that TJ was smart and that I could use his gift of gab to my and my company's benefit. And it worked. TJ managed to charm and dazzle lots of corporate clients, and in the beginning of 2016, we were raking in lots of cash. But TJ was also spending it. TJ never took the train once while in New York. He insisted on Ubers everywhere. If I were invited to an event, he wanted to go too. If I needed a new outfit, he needed one too! When I told him that it was my job to dress up, not his, he would say that I would look crazy if he was standing next to me at an event in subpar clothes. So he went shopping. All the time. With my money.

I wanted him to feel at home, so I obliged his spending. I looked the other way when he took my debit card and bought a $1,500 chain. I tried to ignore it when he started wearing my clothes. We wore the same shoe size, so my gold Margiela sneakers became his Margiela sneakers. Anything vaguely unisex, he would wear. Givenchy t-shirts, designer shoes, and more. He offered to help me with my shoe before heading to an event and I looked down and noticed that my Cartier Love bracelet was on his wrist, and he hadn't asked to wear it. He just took it. When I protested, he said I was being selfish. When I told him we should be saving, he declared that he made the money. It wasn't my money, it was OUR money. It wasn't my company, it was OUR company. I thought to myself: this is my man and I love him. Why should I have a problem sharing if we're going to get married one day? So I looked the other way.

As time wore on in our relationship, I could tell TJ was feeling jealous of me and my success. He tagged along as I spoke to young girls at a high school, encouraging them to go for their dreams. Afterwards I felt triumphant, but all he could tell me is how I misused a vocabulary word. When I balked at his criticism, he insisted he was only saying it to make me better.

He also started doing small things to sabotage me. I invited him to two work conferences where he got into fights with people in attendance. At one conference in LA, he got involved in a fight that had nothing at all to do with him. Some drunk guys were causing trouble with another guy and his girlfriend. TJ jumped into the mix, and defended the lone man who had to take on the group. He looked one aggressor in the eye, and said, "I will beat you to sleep." When I tried to stop him, it was as if his eyes were glazed over. I could not control him. Before he threw the first punch, I left the area, not wanting to be present during the fight or associated with him. He had an issue with abandonment because of his childhood, so made me feel guilty for leaving. When I returned, he insisted all the women around wanted to sleep with him because of his display of force. I doubted it. I was never invited back to the conference again.

It was tricky having him on my team. Because of the public nature of his arrest, he was easy to Google. I had him go by an alias. He offered to change his name, but I told him it was unnecessary. I hated having to lie about him and his name. I hated having to worry about someone googling him and finding out our dirty little secret. But in some cases, he wanted business associates to know about his transgressions, as if he were proud of it. While getting a haircut in Atlanta, he proudly showed off his mugshot to the barber. He encouraged some colleagues to google him. It's as if he were wearing his crime as a badge of honor.

Meanwhile, our romantic relationship was spiraling out of control. We butted heads about finances and about his excessive spending. He'd have his friends and family from Detroit come and stay with us for weeks on end, with us footing the bills for food and transportation. His mother was hitting me up every month for money. His family was taking up court in my home and I paid the rent!

Our fights got more and more intense. One time he wanted me to buy him a plane ticket, and the card we shared didn't have any money on it. He badgered me, as I was asleep early one morning, to buy his ticket. I took my time, got my purse, and got my debit card out when he snatched it from my hands. As I went to grab it back, he yelled, "Fuck You, Bitch," inches away from my face. We tussled over the card, and then I kicked him with all of my force off of the bed. It felt great. He then approached me again and I kicked him again. To his credit, TJ never physically put his hands on me, but as I began to do my research, nagging someone and yelling expletives in their face is definitely a sure sign of abuse.

Then the cheating began. His hometown is known for high school and college football, and most times when we were there, we attended football games for fun. TJ and I decided to go to a game at his alma mater, and thought we were cute in our matching Harvard sweatshirts. A woman called TJ during the game, agitated that he was stepping out with another woman. Apparently we had sat in our cute coupledom in front of her family, and they had called her to tell her of the news. As she yelled at TJ over the phone, she threatened to come to the game and tell me that they were sleeping together. Instead of risk public embarrassment, TJ had me gather our things and leave. For the two seconds on the phone TJ allowed me to speak to her, she revealed that they were in a relationship and that he told her I was strictly a business partner.

Another time, I found a pair of women's Bebe shoes in his car. He found a local crackhead to lie and tell me that the shoes were hers.

I am not a liar and am not used to people lying to me. I failed to see the signs until one day in May.

TJ and I came to share some finances. I didn't want to emasculate him, so we shared the card on one of our bank accounts. He asked for access to the business bank account and I thank GOD to this day I never granted him access. With the card he did have access to, I received alerts every time either of us made a transaction.

He had a court date coming up and told me he was going to Cleveland to see his Cousin Christina and get some much needed emotional support. But the day he was supposedly in Cleveland, I received notifications that a couple transactions were made in Atlanta. I called him on the cell phone I was paying for, and asked, "Are you in Atlanta?" He said that he was. I asked him why he lied, and he said that his Cousin Christina decided last minute to meet him at her house in Atlanta. I called his cousin and asked her "Are you in Georgia?" She replied, "No, I'm at home. " I told TJ what she said, and he lied again, saying that his cousin had a home in Georgia. Then he got a random woman on the street to act as his Cousin Christina on the phone. He just couldn't stop with his lie. And eventually I had to realize that TJ was incapable of telling the truth.

TJ was Harvard educated and brilliant, yes. He had triumphed against many adversities, and seemed normal. But he was a criminal. A con artist. A liar. A cheater. He was scum. And I had had him in the inner sanctum of my home. And he had his hands in my business that I had worked so hard to create.

I told my parents of his Atlanta lie, and it didn't take them long before they got activated. My Dad decided to fly to New York and made sure TJ got out of my house and took his stuff with him. Though it's hard to believe, TJ had found his way back into my heart. He was apologetic and love is blind. But once my Dad came to New York and made him 'take his shit,' I realized a cloud had lifted from me. I felt lighter. I was happier. And I knew that TJ could never ever return.

It took me a while to realize how much I had risked by being with him. All of the fabulous corporate money I was getting would have dried up if I continued to be associated with a criminal. With his volatile nature, absence of self awareness and lack of morals, TJ could have ruined my business. I was so committed to being in love and having a family that I was willing to risk it all.

Little did I know that TJ could not have loved me in any real way because he was fine taking advantage of me. He had no problem stealing my money, wearing everything valuable that I owned, then having his family and friends hit me up for cash as well. He was using me for my wealth and access, all the while ruining several professional relationships that it had taken me years to build.

Any man that loves you shouldn't guilt you into doing things you don't want to do. Any man that loves you shouldn't discourage you or make you feel badly. Any man that loves you wouldn't make you put your career or finances at risk for their benefit.

My friends and parents joined hands around me and made me realize how much I had to lose, how hard I had worked, and ultimately how valuable I am.

Being with TJ taught me to be discerning about who you let in your life. You can think that you're just another girl, living her life, but I had worked hard, crashed gates, gotten blacklisted, sent out newsletters, moved to Paris and back, took risks, grabbed pix with celebrities and that much more to get to where I was. And I couldn't take that for granted or let any man take what I had rightfully earned away from me.

I also couldn't continue to undervalue what I had. It was hard to get into those celebrity parties. It took almost 10 years of hard work to become an ambassador for national brands. Some of TJ's friends called me a sugar mamma because I was making a lot of money and was willing to spend a lot on him because I loved him. But he was using me. Using my kindness for weakness. Preying upon someone who genuinely only wanted the best for him.

People ask me where TJ is now, and the answer is: I don't know and I don't care. I know that he can find me because I am a public figure. But now I have security. I never want to see him again.

And GOD is good. Not even two months after I broke up with TJ, I met up with a designer in LA who wanted to gift me some clothes. I thought I'd be meeting a metrosexual gay man, but I met a tall, handsome chocolate brother and we hit it off. We are now dating and he is everything TJ wasn't. He is truthful, he is kind, and he is supportive. Though he could stand to benefit from my celebrity contacts, he doesn't. When I ask him if he wants to come with me to awards shows or galas, he passes, saying that the situation is 'for me.' He has his own job, his own business, and best of all, he is my biggest supporter.

Though I don't know what the future may hold for us, he has shown me that true love is possible--if you are patient and faithful. You have to be with a man who is not intimidated or envious of your success. You must be equally yoked. Make sure he is worthy of you and brings something to the table. Make sure he is positive and supportive and pushes you to be the best version of yourself you can be.

Have standards for yourself. If you are an honest person, be with someone honest! If you work hard, be with a hard worker. Ask for and pay attention to references. And know that just because someone has a fancy degree or has friends in common with you doesn't mean they're a good person.

Take your time and get to know someone. Truly observe them. Don't look the other way and don't ignore the signs when the writing's on the wall.

Make sure they bring nothing but good things and positivity into your life. You deserve it.

❧ 10 ❧

The New Frontier

THESE DAYS, I'M moreso about focusing on building Fashion Bomb World. We are no longer outsiders, angling to get in. We gained the respect and attention of the people we write about and now it's time to leverage that and create our own movement and media empire.

I've been able to find a group of committed, smart young women and men who have taken over the day-to-day operations of *Fashion Bomb Daily*. I didn't have anyone mentoring me coming up, so I am paying it forward. I give my writers free reign to be creative. They get a wage and maintain the site so that I can expand the Claire Sulmers and The Bomb Life brand.

I am more active as an ambassador for various companies. Though I post the occasional celeb "get the look" outfit, I leave that to my team so I can focus on more lucrative opportunities. Every month, I am speaking on several panels and traveling around the world to host shows and talk about entrepreneurship and embracing your dreams. I am in talks to have a TV show, and hey, look! I'm writing my first book.

Fashion Bomb is diversifying in several ways, from producing exclusive editorials to expanding Fashion Bomb TV.

The blogosphere has changed so much since I started. While it used to be all about websites, now most people are on social media. While it used to be all about YouTube, now we can do what we want on Facebook Live, Snapchat, and Periscope.

If you're looking to get into blogging now, start where you are and with whatever tools you have in your arsenal. Because things are more live and not as edited, it's easy to get started. Facebook Live, Snapchat, Instagram, and even YouTube are creating new stars every day.

Don't Be Scared

Things will never be absolutely perfect. I wish I could embrace this also, especially when it comes to things being perfectly polished! But sometimes you just have to go with it. Purchase a tripod and know that your smartphone can act just like a professional camera.

Creating a blog is free via WordPress, and you can get a theme for less than $200. Starting an Instagram account is also free.

Come to the table with personality, exclusives, and your unique point of view. We are as unique as our DNA and we all have access to different types of resources. Think about what you have, right now, at your disposal, and use it.

People respond well to celebrity. Who do you know that's close to you who can give you insight on a celeb look? Do you know any stylists? Stylist assistants? Start there. Do you know any up-and-coming artists who will be the next big thing? Do you know of any makeup artists doing cool stuff? Start there.

The beauty of being young is that you know what's hot now and what will be hot next. What are your friends obsessed with? What are all the high school kids doing? Start there.

But although you know a lot about what's new, you don't know everything. Many millennials believe that because you can create your own enterprise with a computer, Wifi, and a dream, you don't have to work hard. You can learn a lot from paying your dues and observing successful people in your industry. If you want to blog, learn how to write. If you want to do video, intern at a TV station. There is a chance you are blessed with natural talent, and that's great. But we can always get better. The great thing about starting small and interning is that you can network. A lot of my best friends and supporters started off in journalism, like me. A lot of articles I was featured in coming up were because of friendships I had made over the years. Bigger corporations always have more access to events, resources, and contacts simply because they've been around longer and have a track record. Use those resources to your benefit, and when the time is right, leave and do your own thing.

Also: Study. There are loads of resources at your fingertips. Hop online. Visit your local library.

Listen to talks on YouTube. The digital landscape is vast and the world is your oyster.

When It's Time to Leave Your Job

I am not a corporate girl. I hate dressing up, waking up, and working for someone else! But in the days before *Fashion Bomb Daily* was profitable, I had to pay the bills. I remember staring out of the window as planes flew overhead, wishing I was on that plane instead of trudging another day to work. If I could do it again, I would have planned my exit properly. I would have saved a large portion of each paycheck and made sure I had a nice cushion before sending in my resignation. But I didn't. You can't be successful without planning, so try your best to be as organized and responsible as possible.

I realized it was time to go when I couldn't ignore my true passion anymore. I knew I wanted to do more than be a fact checker. My dreams wouldn't allow me to go to work another day. So I quit. When it's time to quit is a very personal decision, but I urge you not to wait too long or to try to find the perfect moment.

When I moved to Paris, absolutely nothing was planned, and I suffered as a result. But if I hadn't started where I was with what I had, I wouldn't be where I am today. Try to plan as best you can, then just go for it. You won't get anything accomplished if you procrastinate. Start today and do one thing every day that will push you closer to your dreams.

Building a Team

Fashion Bomb Daily has had interns since 2007. One of our first interns, Vuitton, is still writing with us several years later! Though Vuitton is fabulous, *Fashion Bomb Daily* has had dozens of interns! Sometimes people think they want to work but don't realize how much work it is. Some people are only in it to meet celebrities or go to events. (Tip: You won't be going to any events until you've proven your devotion to the brand, and that takes a while). All that to say, while some people you bring on board are great, some aren't so great. Such is life.

Having a great team is essential, especially if you want your business to scale. Though we all wish to be superwomen, we physically can't do it all. It's impossible! You have to get a great team in place, but doing so takes trial and error.

Some people will do everything right and show their commitment and talent. Other people won't. Get rid of the riff raff and hold on tight to the good ones.

Fashion Bomb Daily now has five to ten independent contractors who do everything from updating our Facebook page to pinning on our Pinterest accounts and maintaining Instagram. I am so busy building the Claire brand that I don't have time to be on Instagram all day. Find people who are willing to invest in you and your brand so that it can grow.

If you value your team, treat them with respect. Say thank you. Pay them. Talk to them. If they're having a personal issue, make sure they feel like they can come to you. Acknowledge their birthdays. Offer them perks. *Fashion Bomb Daily* staffers have attended awards shows, helped out with photo shoots, received swag, and popped into exclusive events. Show your team you value them in concrete ways.

I'm tremendously loyal, so I'd rather have a small group of people who will work extremely hard over several people who are mediocre. I try my best to teach people, offer constructive feedback, and motivate them.

Being a great leader is a learned trait, and figuring out what works for your organization will take time also. But once you have mastered how to be a great leader, your team will stick with you through the end.

Dress the Part

If you want to work in fashion, please understand that it is a superficial business and looks matter. You don't necessarily have to be pretty or handsome, though that definitely helps! If you haven't been blessed with good looks, don't fret.

Get your makeup done. Get your hair done. Get a manicure/pedicure. Take care of your skin and your body. Work out. Drink water.

If you are not naturally fashionable, there are stylists everywhere. Everyone wants to be a stylist these days! Identify a girl you know who always looks bomb and get her to help you out. If everyone loves your look, great! If people are dragging you with every camera click, switch it up! The people will let you know if you're Hot! Or Hmm...trust me.

Network, Network, Network

If you live in a city like New York, you know there are parties every night. You can't make them all, but make the ones you deem strategic. If you're looking to go in a luxurious direction, jump at the opportunity to go to a party sponsored by a luxury brand. Understand that these are opportunities that could lead to sponsorship or strategic partnerships. It is not enough to write about things from behind your computer. You will increase your opportunities by 100% if you go out and meet people in your industry.

Going to parties by yourself can be difficult, but once you go to a few, you'll start to notice a few familiar faces. If you're stumped, go to the bar, then strike up a conversation with someone who looks friendly. If you're having an awful time, you don't have to stay! Identify the publicist in the room, thank them for inviting you, and promise to follow up. Make sure you make contact with whoever is of import in the room (publicist, anyone working for the brand, host, celebrity), before making your exist. If you really want to connect with the brand, do a recap of the event on your website or social media. Every little bit helps.

Fine-tuning Your Social Media Profile

Social media is the new currency, so it would serve you best to pay attention.

Pictures say a thousand words, so make sure every picture on your feed is crisp, clean, and gorgeous. Study other feeds you like and see what they do and how you can improve upon it.

For Instagram, I focus on the Rule of 3. So every three pictures have the same composition or background, or tell the same story. When someone looks at your feed in grid form, you want everything to look like one cohesive, beautiful story.

Some influencers use iPhone pictures, but I prefer to use professional pictures. Find someone young, hungry, and talented who is willing to work with you. You both can grow together.

If your goal is to work with corporate clients like Toyota, Reebok, etc., keep it classy. Understand that your feed is not a place for you to let everything hang out. This is not fun; this is work. Treat it accordingly. If you absolutely must share pictures from your booze-filled love fest on Instagram, consider having a private profile.

If you are a designer, your business feed should feature looks of pieces from your brand. Consider shooting a lookbook with a professional model, photographer, and hairstylist. Don't put pictures of yourself unless you are the ideal model for the clothes. Do not post selfies or anything personal on your business page if you are the owner of a clothing or accessories brand.

Try to avoid using filters or collages. You want your Instagram feed to look like pages of a catalogue from a high-end department store.

Politics and fashion can go hand in hand. If you feel strongly about something, say it. But also realize that sometimes political discussions can alienate customers. Tread lightly but also realize you do not live in a bubble.

Maintain certain quality standards for whatever you put out in the world. This also goes for how you dress when you go out on the street.

I don't always wear makeup, but on those occasions I don't, I am wearing a pair of popping sunglasses with lipstick. I try to make sure I have a nice bag and look put together. You will never see me, not even in the airport, in pajamas or anything dirty or unappealing. You are a brand ambassador at all times, so act accordingly. This extends to parties.

Party Time

In the entertainment and fashion industry, you will be invited to events that look like parties. There will be an open bar, dope music, and loads of fun people! Do not think you are at a party with your friends. It is business.

Don't get too drunk. Don't dance with wild abandon. Don't slosh over to a celebrity and annoy them by asking them to get on their Snapchat. Just be cool.

How to Act Around Celebrities

When it comes to celebrities, I'd say feel the situation out. I've taken pictures with lots of celebrities. Most times they were in public places, or at parties and events where lots of picture taking was going on.

I recently was blessed to go backstage for the Beyoncé concert, and I met Queen Bey herself! We had to go through many layers of security to reach her. And when we saw her, she had just emerged from a relaxing massage. She was in comfortable clothes, no makeup. She just looked simple (and effortlessly gorgeous, obviously!). Though I would have DIED to get a picture with her, it wasn't the right time. If she was dressed with all her hair, makeup, and sequins, then yes. But that time just wasn't the right time.

Later on backstage, Jay Z came through and Blue Ivy was running around. Getting all of this on Snapchat would have been GOLDEN, but I felt like it just wasn't appropriate. No one else had their phones out. Everyone was just chillin', and Jay Z is known to not take pictures. It's not his thing. And with children, you also have to be very careful. So I just sat down, had a glass of D'USSÉ, and chilled. There comes a point with celebrities when you are in the room because you're supposed to be there. You're not a fan. You're not a journalist or a scheming blogger looking for dirt. You are a colleague. And you should act like you're supposed to be there. If in doubt, just look at how other people are acting, and act like them!

I've actually met the Carters before, years ago. I shook their hands and kept it moving. If the spirit hits you, go for it. If you're on a red carpet, or at any after party and they are taking lots of pics, go crazy. But there might come a time when you've already taken 25 selfies, and now it's time to talk. When it's time to talk, have something to talk about. These people are powerful. You won't always have their attention. Ask them for advice. See how you can work together. Ask for their thoughts on anything that would enrich you. Ask them to follow you on Instagram! Ask for their phone number. If I had a chance to talk to Beyoncé, I'd ask for an interview and to feature her in an editorial shoot. With Jay Z, I'd probably ask for business advice. If he wasn't familiar with *Fashion Bomb Daily*, I would make sure he was.

A lot of times people of that caliber have heard it all before. You know you are special and we know your mom thinks you're the bomb, but don't be discouraged if their eyes don't light up. When you meet someone, just plant a seed. I met Gayle King three times before she remembered who I was. I had taken at least four pictures with Kanye West before his manager, Don C, recalled who I was. Another big no-no when it comes to celebrities or anyone who might meet a lot of people all the time is to ask, "Do you remember me?" They meet millions of people all the time! Perhaps you weren't memorable. And don't be offended if you are not memorable! Keep introducing yourself until they have a reason to remember you.

If you want to be taken seriously, there is a point when you no longer act like a fan. Act like you're supposed to be there. Be cool. If you make a celebrity feel uncomfortable or do anything that makes them feel as if you violated their privacy, you may never be invited back again.

Also, don't be a gossip! Some bloggers might think it's cute to spill the tea for some page views. That is the first step to your industry expulsion. Hanging around stylists and celebrities, I have heard lots and lots of juicy gossip. LOTS! It will never get to *TMZ* or anything of the sort. Respect people's privacy. Understand that celebrities are people, too! They have feelings. They have a reputation to protect. Know that what goes around, comes around, so always do the right thing. You will increase your shelf life exponentially if you learn how to keep it professional, cool, and prudent.

Don't Burn Bridges

I had a writer once who I sent on a press trip. I'll be honest, I didn't really want to go, so I threw the option out to my staff to see who was willing. He was the first to volunteer.

While there, he apparently acted badly. He wasn't social, and instead of interacting with others on the trip, he sullenly listened to his Beats by Dre headphones. Usually the deal with press trips is that you are supposed to write something about your experience. But when it came time for him to post his recap, he was silent. I called him, texted him, and emailed him with no response.

I got my response when I saw an article, penned by him, on another site. He was discussing his awful experience on the press trip. The people in charge of sending him were colleagues of mine and they were pissed. I wrote him a note, expressing my dismay and telling him that what he did was reprehensible. Instead of apologize, he said, "Thanks for the note." I fired him immediately.

Don't be shortsighted when it comes to your job and reputation. People talk, and your reputation is everything. Guard it with your life.

This Is a Creative Industry, so Create!

When I first started writing, I wanted to work for *Elle* or *Vogue*, and thought that just having a job there would mean that people would tell me what to write about. In some cases that is true, but in a creative industry, you have to create your own path. In magazines and websites, you have to pitch compelling ideas. No one is going to give you those ideas, you have to create the ideas yourself. Perhaps get a good friend or advisor to hear your ideas to figure out the best one, and go for it.

Many young people come up to me, asking me what they should write about or what their blog should be about. That is not up for me to decide. You have to tap your imagination and background to see what unique thing you have to offer to the world.

Create your own TV show. Create your own podcast or webinar. People will make suggestions to you. Filter those out, too! Trust your intuition and know that you are the only person who can make it happen.

Also know that art does not exist in a vacuum. So once you do something great, let the world know.

Collect emails from people you know and create a newsletter or a mailing list. Create a separate email list for other websites or Instagram sites you'd like to link to you. Reach out to people. Get their contact information and stay in touch. Plant seeds.

Listen to feedback. If no one is reading or leaving comments, maybe you're not doing the best thing for the people. My dream was always to be on TV, so of course I was excited to do interview for *Fashion Bomb*'s YouTube channel. I'll admit it: I wasn't great! Though I think I'm bubbly and fun in person, I seemed boring and dead on camera. And people told me so! One reader suggested I just quit cold turkey. Someone else suggested I just sit things out and let someone else take over Fashion Bomb TV — something I created! I could have ignored their suggestions and shrugged them off as haters (some probably were), but instead of quit or get someone to take my job, I got to work. My first step was to go to a group acting class, which was fun. I now have an acting coach, whom I visit before I do any on-air work. She is expensive at $200 an hour, but she is worth every penny! And by working with her, I have been able to secure on-air gigs for something other than Fashion Bomb TV! I've been featured on BET and VH1, and been booked to cover red carpets for galas and awards shows. If you're not good at something, take a class and get better!

There is a fine line between listening to criticism and wholly changing yourself to please other people. You have to decide what is reasonable for you. For years, readers told me I was obese, so I lost weight. They said I couldn't dress, so I refined my look. Now, some have said I should cut my hair and go for a straight, sleek look. But I like my hair, so I'll keep it! Who knows, perhaps I would have reached greater heights more quickly if I had a long weave, but I don't care. My locs are my signature, and I am happy to be "nappy." So my hair stays. I will never bleach my skin or touch my face because I love my skin and think I'm a pretty decent-looking person! So many celebrities fall into a trap of listening to criticism to the point where they ruin their face and body. You have to have a reality check as well. Sometimes the thing people talk the most about is your most endearing trait! Just know that if you want to be the people's choice, i.e. popular, you will have to conform just a bit, whether that means getting better at something or tweaking your look. I'd say, however: Don't lose your individuality. A world where everyone is exactly the same is boring. Find your best qualities and make them better, all while staying true to yourself, what you value, and what you love.

Also understand that things take time. It is only after 10 years that I'm starting to truly enjoy the fruits of my labor. There were many lean years when I could only afford shoes that would break on me as I was walking down 5th Avenue!

When I lived in Paris, I wrote down that I wanted a pair of Christian Louboutin black pumps. By the end of my time in France, those Louboutins were mine. Once you achieve a goal, set a new one. My goal was to live full time from my website. To make six figures. I've done all that, and now I've created a vision board, to own a private jet and live a multi-million dollar lifestyle full of mansions, champagne, diamonds, luxury cars, and designer bags. Don't be shy about praying or asking the Universe for what you want.

You have the power in your brain and at the end of your fingertips to create the life that you want.
Set concrete goals.
Write them down.
Put them somewhere you can see them when you wake up and go to sleep.
Tell anyone who will listen of your sometimes outrageous plans.
Reach for the stars.
You'll be surprised how many of your dreams and goals come true.

Letters to my Younger Self

Dear Claire,

Take yourself seriously from the get go. Purchase the URL TheFashionBomb.com when you can. Get a Tax ID number and separate your business expenses from personal expenses.

Handle your business.

Pay your taxes. As soon as you even make $1,000, pay your taxes. Take a business class or a finance class if you are not good with money. Link with a financial advisor or a CPA. Get a savings account, an investment account, and a retirement account and start saving.

You don't want to look up one day and have nothing to show for all of your hard work. Be meticulous about how you spend money.

Budget. Keep track of your expenses. See what you are spending too much money on and think of ways to cut back. Make sure you are aware of how and where you spend your money. Do not spend frivolously.

Get a financial advisor who is invested in your success because they know that your success is their success. Invest in yourself and your happiness.

———⟫●⟪———

Dear Claire,

Love will come at the perfect time — when you are ready. Don't worry about it. The perfect man exists for you. Yes, you should date and have fun, but don't become too attached to the idea of being in a romantic relationship. Don't cling to the wrong person because you think that you're a black woman and that things are hard out there. Don't believe the negative propaganda. There are men out there for you. Good men, who don't cheat, have great jobs, are respectful, and treat you like the queen you are. There are men out there who will invest in you and your dreams and push you to be your greatest self.

Do not stay with a man if he puts your down and makes you feel less than beautiful. Do not stay with a man if he yells in your face and calls you a bitch. Do not stay with a man if he cheats on you.

Do not stay with a man if you feel the need to check his phone and email. Think twice if a man does not have close friends and if he has a shady source of income. Think twice if your mom, friends, and family don't like him!

You deserve the man who will want to support you and your dreams. You deserve the man who will give you everything you deserve. And he exists. Do not settle for less than the best, especially when it comes to the man you will be intimate with.

Take your time choosing your mate, as this might be one of the most important decisions you ever make in life. The best mate can drive you the highest heights and the wrong mate can drag you down. Don't let it happen.

Be careful of the people you let in your life. Make sure everyone around you shares your values. That they are people of their word. Good people, who only want the best for you. Beware of hangers on and leeches. Beware of associating yourself with people who might besmirch your name and take away from your shine. If someone does something that does not sit well with you, trust your gut and your intuition. Know that there are some people out to hurt you, but there are also people out here to help you. But sometimes you have to get rid of the hurt to get to the help.

———➤●◄———

Dear Claire,

Sometimes not getting what you want is a tremendous blessing. Sometimes you want something SO BAD. You pray for it, wish for it, and even write it down. But if it doesn't come to pass, let it go, and know that GOD has greater plans for you.

If you had gotten those jobs at *Marie Claire* and *Elle*, you wouldn't have pushed yourself to move to Paris. If you had been hired by *Vogue*, you wouldn't have created your own *Vogue*.

Know that every shut door will open a window for a new opportunity. If you had gotten hired at Paris *Vogue*, you wouldn't have moved back to New York and enjoyed tremendous success. Set goals, but stay flexible. Sometimes you make plans and GOD laughs. Everything eventually works out for the best.

Trust your gut. Read between the lines and watch the signs. Stay open-minded, flexible, and humble. Work hard and do what you love. Know when to hold fast to a dream, and be open to letting it go, knowing that something better is poised to come your way.

———➤●◄———

Dear Claire,

Your hard work will pay off. One day. Those nights you stayed up writing so much your eyes turned red and your wrists ached. Those days when you spent hours on a post to receive zero comments. It's OK. One day it will all pay off.

Success doesn't happen overnight, and you shouldn't expect your success to happen overnight. You get the glamour after the grunt work. You have to put work in. Sometimes you make mistakes and missteps, but don't be discouraged. Keep pushing.

There comes a point when the world steps in to help you. If you invest your time and energy, and people recognize you are serious about what you are doing, they will support you.

———➤●◄———

Dear Claire,

Be disciplined. Plan. Because you create your own way, you have no one to rely upon but yourself. You have to determine when you wake up how much you work, and ultimately how successful you are.

Be very careful with your time. Proper planning prevents piss poor performance. Give yourself time to plan but also realize that when it's time to go, GO. If you plan properly you can avoid those moments of struggle and anxiety.

Half of the battle is showing up, so make sure you show up to your appointments, on time. Go over and above. Give the best of yourself in everything you do. You receive in proportion to what you give to the world.

———⟫●◆⟪———

Dear Claire,

Diversify your offerings. Don't just have a website, do video, podcasts, Snapchat, Instagram, Facebook, Pinterest, and everything else!

Use your platform to empower in many ways, from panels to networking events to exclusive editorials and experiences.

You have to start somewhere, so not everything will be perfect from jump.

Your first Cocktails with Claire was in a small boutique with 20 people max and your boyfriend serving vodka in paper cups. Your latest event was in a venue that held 400 people and had a musical performance. Start somewhere and continue to build.

Also, don't be afraid to share your story with the world, even the most painful and vulnerable parts. You never know who you may be encouraging by your testimony.

———⟶•⟵———

Dear Claire,

You are a survivor. You have slept on top of tubs and been down to your last two dollars. And in those moments, GOD showered you with grace, and found you friends who fed you when you were hungry, and gave you shelter when you had nowhere else to go.

You have dealt with adversaries, some who went over and above trying to ruin your career and reputation. GOD don't like ugly and karma is a bitch. Though some may seem to be winning at the moment, the wicked shall never prosper.

You are capable of surviving the worst. And perhaps know that GOD is showing you the very worst so that you can appreciate the very best.

Know that GOD has your back when you step out on Faith. Of course, plan. But even when things are their absolute worst, know that GOD will provide you with the basics. He will walk with you and will never abandon you.

Dear Claire,

The sky is the limit. Do not limit yourself by what you think is possible or practical. Everything you ask for, you will receive. Stay positive. Avoid gossip. Avoid saying or thinking anything negative. Thoughts become things, so make sure you choose the best thoughts.

Create a vision board full of whatever you may want. We are as unique as our DNA, so what you want is yours and yours alone.

Use your imagination.

Dream of yourself accepting an award in front of a large crowd of your peers. Then think about what the award is for. Think about every last detail until it happens.

Write your Wikipedia page full of what you would have liked to have accomplished by the end of your career. Include the most minute detail and shower yourself with gifts and blessings.

Don't be afraid to dream big.

———⟫●⟪———

Dear Claire,

Don't be discouraged. Things will get hard. Vendors won't pay on time. Sometimes invoices will pile up. Sometimes you aren't motivated. Sometimes you won't want to get out of bed. Take a day or an hour to feel sorry for yourself, then get up. Everyone gets down. Everyone fears failure. You will succeed if you persist. So get up. And go forth.

Look around you. Most of your peers will quit. Most of them will think things are too difficult and wave the white flag. Sometimes it's not about who is the best, it's about who is the last one standing.

Think of everyone who will rejoice if you quit. If you decide not to go for what you want in life. Don't give them the satisfaction. Don't allow them to win.

Live by the phrase: I will not lose.

———⟫●⟪———

Dear Claire,

I love you. I love your smooth, gorgeous skin. I love your bright eyes and smile. I love your style. Your flair. Your sense of humor. I love that you know when to work hard and when to play hard. You are brilliant, talented, and driven, and the world deserves to know that.

I pray that you feel that love for yourself, and know that everything comes from within.

You have everything you need to be all you can be in the world.

———————

Dear Claire,

You've got this. You are smart, talented, and driven. Don't be scared. Don't worry as much. Don't take things personally. Know that not everyone is going to be on your side, but that's OK. As long as you believe fiercely in yourself, you'll be OK.

———————

Dear Claire,

Don't be so hard on yourself. You're great.

Sometimes you will fall short. It's OK. Pick yourself back up and try again.

Whatever you are not the best at, you can learn. Read books, take classes, and watch videos.

If at first you don't succeed, try and try again.

The most successful people are the most confident, not the most competent. So believe in yourself first, then the world will follow.